Economic Globalisation and the Environment

ORGANISATION FOR ECONOMIC CO-OPERATION AND DEVELOPMENT

ORGANISATION FOR ECONOMIC CO-OPERATION AND DEVELOPMENT

Pursuant to Article 1 of the Convention signed in Paris on 14th December 1960, and which came into force on 30th September 1961, the Organisation for Economic Co-operation and Development (OECD) shall promote policies designed:

- to achieve the highest sustainable economic growth and employment and a rising standard of living in Member countries, while maintaining financial stability, and thus to contribute to the development of the world economy;
- to contribute to sound economic expansion in Member as well as non-member countries in the process of economic development; and
- to contribute to the expansion of world trade on a multilateral, non-discriminatory basis in accordance with international obligations.

The original Member countries of the OECD are Austria, Belgium, Canada, Denmark, France, Germany, Greece, Iceland, Ireland, Italy, Luxembourg, the Netherlands, Norway, Portugal, Spain, Sweden, Switzerland, Turkey, the United Kingdom and the United States. The following countries became Members subsequently through accession at the dates indicated hereafter: Japan (28th April 1964), Finland (28th January 1969), Australia (7th June 1971), New Zealand (29th May 1973), Mexico (18th May 1994), the Czech Republic (21st December 1995), Hungary (7th May 1996), Poland (22nd November 1996) and the Republic of Korea (12th December 1996). The Commission of the European Communities takes part in the work of the OECD (Article 13 of the OECD Convention).

Publié en français sous le titre :

MONDIALISATION ÉCONOMIQUE ET ENVIRONNEMENT

FOREWORD

OECD Environment Ministers recognise both the challenges and the opportunities that economic globalisation represents for the environment. This is why, meeting in Paris in February 1996, they asked the OECD Secretariat to undertake ... "a thorough assessment of the relationships between globalisation and environmental policies, including pollution prevention and control and the sustainable use of natural resources, drawing on the full range of the Organisation's capabilities and on-going work. The aim is to deepen understanding of the linkages between environmental policies and structural issues, including competitiveness, employment, investment, trade and technology, and of the extent to which policy developments in these areas promote the internalisation of environmental costs. A report should be presented to the OECD Council Ministerial in 1997."

This publication responds to that mandate. It begins by introducing the main elements of the economic globalisation process, including a framework for linking these elements to changes in environmental conditions. It then examines recent trends in each of these elements, and how each may be actually affecting the environment. The Council of the OECD agreed to the derestriction of this report on May 26, 1997.

TABLE OF CONTENTS

EXECUTIVE SUMMARY

INTRODUCTION

It is generally agreed that economic activity is becoming more "globalised", but there is less agreement about what this will actually mean for the average citizen. Opinions are therefore divided about whether globalisation will ultimately be good or bad overall for society.

Those in favour of globalisation see the benefits mostly in economic terms (especially the increased volume of world output, incomes and employment). Those opposed see the costs primarily in social equity terms (especially the altered distribution of world output, incomes and employment). As always, the policy challenge will be to find ways of realising most of the benefits, while avoiding most of the costs.

Economic globalisation is defined here as a *process* in which the structures of *economic markets, technologies,* and *communication patterns* become progressively more international over time. In general, globalisation should contribute to the expansion of world economic output (*scale effects*). It will also generate shifts in the composition and location of production and consumption activities (*structural effects*). More specifically, different technology paths will be promoted (*technology effects*), and different product mixes will be produced and consumed (*product effects*).

Given that significant market failures already occur within domestic economies, these failures will be even harder to deal with in a more globalised economic context, unless adequate governance structures are in place to deal with them.

This book explores economic globalisation from the particular perspective of the *environment*. Its premise is that globalisation is altering the context of environmental problems at the local, national, regional, and global levels. This is generating new concerns about the development and implementation of environmental policy. It is also opening up new opportunities to promote environmental objectives via the re-orientation of both economic and environmental policies.

Each of the scale, structural, technology, and product effects generated by the globalisation process will also generate environmental effects. Some of these effects may be harmful for the environment; others may be beneficial. It is the *net* environmental effect that is ultimately of most interest.

Economic *globalisation* is a different concept from that of economic *growth*. Globalisation contributes to economic growth, but is only one contributor. Population growth, natural resource endowments, cultural heritage, etc. also play important roles. However, it is difficult to quantify precisely what proportion of total economic growth can be attributed specifically to the globalisation process. Similarly, globalisation will have impacts on the broader goal of *sustainable development*, but will again be only one of the determinants of progress toward this goal.

Analysing the environmental consequences of globalisation must be done over a longer time frame than is required for many economic issues. This is essentially because the economic benefits of policy changes typically appear much sooner than the environmental benefits do. A *dynamic* and *long-term* approach to analysing these environmental effects is therefore required.

There is considerable uncertainty about the long-term ability of the environment to withstand the pressures of even the current *level* of economic activity, let alone the level that might exist in a continuously globalising economy. On the other hand, globalisation may also open up opportunities for *structural and/or technological* changes that could help in the search for solutions over the longer-term.

However, relying on long-term payoffs from structural/technological improvements would be a risky strategy from the environmental perspective. The main source of this risk is that the long-term environmental consequences of today's economic behaviour are poorly understood. This implies that the environmental effects of globalisation *cannot* be viewed strictly through the lens of *today's* economic interests. A "precautionary approach" is therefore required, to take account for the possibility that current perceptions about future environmental conditions may turn out to be wrong (and perhaps, *very* wrong). On the other hand, the actual level of "precaution" to be applied, as well as the particular instruments to be used in implementing this approach, both need to be clearly thought out.

GOVERNANCE

Globalisation will reduce the ability of national governments to act *unilaterally*. Not only will the decisions of individual governments have less impact on globalised markets, there will also be increased pressure on governments not to imperil the competitive position of their own constituents by taking unilateral action.

Globalisation intensifies pressures for both economic performance and economic policies in different countries to become more alike (*e.g. market convergence*). The deeper and broader the level of market integration, the greater these tendencies will be. In addition, the larger the share of a given country in global trade and capital flows, the greater the forces of convergence will be toward the economic policies *of that nation*.

OECD countries are simultaneously the "large-market" countries, and the most highly integrated ones. Convergence is therefore likely to occur both within the OECD group, as well as from the developing countries toward the OECD.

The same forces leading to *economic* policy convergence also work in the direction of *environmental* policy convergence. *Some* environmental product and production standards are therefore likely to converge around an "OECD average", as well as around industry-wide averages (in the case of internationally-exposed industries).

This implies that what the OECD group does to address the environmental problems associated with globalisation will matter a lot. In this regard, *OECD "leadership"* will be critical. It also suggests that the policy reaction of an individual OECD country to the environmental consequences of globalisation is likely to be "conditioned" mostly by policies adopted by its major trading partners (generally, the other OECD countries), rather than by policies adopted in the eveloping ones.

OECD environmental policy innovations may therefore be constrained by the need to obtain agreement among its major trading partners. In the absence of such agreement, environmental policy innovations may tend to converge around the *status quo*. Unfortunately, maintaining the *status quo* may not be enough to address the full range of environmental problems that could be associated with globalisation.

Market-driven policy convergence will *reduce* competitiveness problems, but will not *eliminate* them. Competitiveness issues will still "condition" the required environmental policy response. In addition, market-based policy responses might not even be sufficient to address the *ecological* bases of globalisation/environment problems. This is because: *i)* markets often do not capture environmental externalities at all; *ii)* even where they *do* capture some of these externalities, markets are typically not sensitive to *local* ecological conditions; and *iii)* countries have even less reason to use markets as a vehicle for internalising transfrontier/global externalities than they do for internalising domestic ones.

For all these reasons, some form of *government* intervention will continue to be necessary in a more globalised economy. The precise form that this intervention should take will depend on the particular circumstances at hand. From the perspective of *economic efficiency*, any such intervention should be made at the same level as the externality itself – thus, local externalities should generally be addressed by local responses; global ones should generally be addressed at the global level. (Of course, other policy goals besides economic efficiency, such as *environmental effectiveness* or *distributive issues*, are often at stake, and could alter this principle n certain situations).

In a more globalised economy, the boundaries between *environmental* effects (externalities) and *economic* effects (especially competitiveness problems) will become less distinct. In addition, local environmental effects will increasingly have international economic consequences, and global environmental problems will generate local economic impacts. This implies that there may be no such thing as a truly "national" environmental externality.

If this is so, at least three types of government intervention may be warranted: *i)* national policies to internalise the environmental costs of those domestic externalities which have *no* international competitiveness implications; *ii)* co-operative arrangements with other governments on common policies to address those *domestic* environmental externalities which *do* have international competitiveness implications; and *iii)* co-operative arrangements with other governments on common policies for addressing transfrontier/global environmental externalities.

The first case involves only national policies, and is not dealt with further here. The latter two cases imply some form of *multilateral co-operation* aimed at resolving environmental problems. This co-operation would have several defining characteristics: *i)* it would not necessarily target international environmental externalities: it could also cover *domestic* externalities where significant international competitiveness concerns exist; *ii)* it would not only involve environmental interests, indeed, the reasons for the co-operation in the first place would often be related to competitiveness (*i.e.* economic) problems, more than to environmental ones; *iii)* it would not necessarily involve all countries. Many environmental (and competitiveness) problems have more relevance at the regional scale than they do at the global level. Even in the particular case of *global* environmental issues, international co-operation might be more efficient if it were organised at the sub-global level, given the significant transaction costs that can be associated with involving a larger number of countries.

International co-operation of the type suggested here could take various forms (*e.g.* voluntary actions, codes of conduct, guidelines, formal agreements, etc.). A few areas in which any or all of these different forms might be considered for future initiatives by the OECD include:

- New opportunities may exist for reducing globalisation-induced *environmental* problems in the context of regional *economic* groupings, such as APEC EU, NAFTA, the OECD itself, etc. These arrangements would build on the strength of the consensus-building approach, and would explicitly work toward the integration of competitiveness *and* environmental issues.

- Opportunities probably exist for improved integration of the competitiveness/financial and environmental objectives of key international organisations (UNEP, World Bank, EBRD, etc.).

- A voluntary "community partnership" approach might be further developed at the *international level*. Such an approach would build on the common interests of governments, the international business community, and community groups with international interests.

- Opportunities may exist for improving the ability of the developing countries to adopt and absorb new *technologies*, as well as to set in place the institutional capability to foster environmentally-friendly innovations themselves ("capacity-building").

- A whole new set of statistics, basic data, and indicators will likely to be needed in the future at the *global* level, to complement existing data and information initiatives at the *national* level.

COMPETITIVENESS

Competitiveness issues lie at the core of the globalisation-environment relationship. Some see environmental policy as a *threat* to competitiveness. This view implies both that more stringent environmental policies will impose unacceptable economic hardships (an *economic* concern), or that pressure will grow to reduce the strength and/or effectiveness of environmental policies (an *environmental* concern).

There is no clear empirical evidence that high (or even relatively high) environmental standards are having a *systematically* negative impact on competitiveness, either at the macroeconomic or the microeconomic level. Most available studies show *insignificant* relationships between the stringency of environmental standards and economic competitiveness, at least in the ways that these variables are usually measured.

For example, some recent studies *have* found the predicted negative correlation between *trade flows* and environmental stringency (especially at the more disaggregated levels of analysis). However, this negative correlation is usually small, and it tends to vary by industry (the structure of individual markets plays a key role), and by time. Conversely, other studies have actually found *positive* correlations between environmental stringency and competitiveness under certain conditions.

Even in cases where a negative relationship *does* seem to occur, it should be recalled that the existence of correlation does not necessarily imply "causality". For example, there are shifts being observed in the trade flows of pollution-intensive products in certain industries and certain countries. However, these shifts are usually better explained by changes in other variables (*e.g.* industry structure, relationships with governments, behaviour of foreign rivals, etc.), than they are by changes in environmental policy itself.

This being the case, it is *not* obvious *a priori* that reducing the stringency (or the enforcement) of environmental regulations would be a very effective way of improving economic competitiveness. On the contrary, many firms are becoming increasingly aware that pollution and the over-use of natural resources is a sign that their existing economic processes are inefficient. Reduced emissions and/or resource usage are therefore increasingly being perceived as opportunities for businesses to actually *improve* their economic competitiveness.

"POLLUTION HAVENS"

National governments are especially sensitive about competitiveness issues at the *international* level. International competitiveness is often judged on the basis of *current* levels of trade, investment, or output. Policy initiatives that threaten these variables are often seen as *reducing* the ability of the nation-state to compete on the international stage. Environmental policy is one of the areas often suspected of contributing to this problem.

Leaving aside the issue of whether national environmental policies may be too low, even to adequately protect a country's own citizens (with the result that national welfare may also be too low), there is the important additional question of whether or not differences in environmental standards cause firms to move their production (and associated employment) to countries with lower *effective* environmental standards (*i.e.* to "pollution havens").

Several observations can be made in response to this question. First, there is little empirical evidence indicating that countries lower their environmental standards, in order to attract "dirty" industries. Nor is there much evidence of firms actually relocating to countries with low environmental standards, in order to take advantage of these lower standards. Many firms *do* move from high- to low-standard jurisdictions, but the *reason* they do so usually has little to do with the level of environmental standards existing in either country. Very few companies invest overseas with reduced environmental compliance costs as their primary goal.

Contrary to what the "pollution haven" hypothesis would predict, the share of OECD investments going into pollution-intensive industries in the developing countries is *not* disproportionately high. On the other hand, there *is* some evidence of a correlation between the degree of "openness-to-trade" in a national economy and the pollution-intensity of the investments it receives – and this relationship is actually *negative*. It may therefore be that the more *open* the economy, the *cleaner* the environmental investments it can expect to receive.

Although there is no *general* support for the "pollution haven" hypothesis there are *some* examples of firms, especially those facing higher-than-average pollution control costs, moving abroad to take advantage of lower costs (including lower costs due to lower environmental standards, or to lower levels of enforcement). Again, however, this should usually be seen as part of the structural adjustment process, and *not* be used as an argument for retaining sub-optimal levels of environmental protection.

On the other hand, the *threat* of industrial relocation is often used by firms in *all* industries who would like to have the burden of environmental policies reduced on their operations. This threat is sometimes real enough to convince policy-makers not to impose new environmental regulations, or to reduce the ones which already exist. In effect, the *threat* of industrial migration based on "pollution havens" (rather than the *reality* of this migration) may be generating a "political drag' on environmental policy-innovations in OECD countries.

FOREIGN INVESTMENT

While North-North capital flows continue to far outpace North-South ones, the non-OECD countries receive a significant (and growing) share of global FDI. A small number of countries, however, are receiving most of the non-OECD FDI. Between 1989 and 1994, 60% of FDI going to non-OECD countries went to Asia, and 27% went to Latin America. A mere 6% went to Africa.

Evidence suggests that foreign investors more often meet the environmental standards of the countries in which they operate than domestic companies do. This reflects the fact that foreign investors often anticipate being subjected to a greater degree of scrutiny than local companies.

Privatisation (a major magnet for FDI in many countries) can yield significant environmental *benefits*, especially in situations where adequate environmental controls are in place. Privatised companies are often better managed, and therefore more concerned about reducing waste and pollution. Where environmental controls are *not* adequate, however, privatisation can open up new opportunities for firms to *reduce* their environmental effort, because their activities would then be subject to lower levels of public sector control.

Pollution liability rules also make a significant difference to the choice of FDI destinations. In Central and Eastern Europe, for example, there is evidence that potential investors have been deterred by the possibility that they will be liable for cleaning up toxic contamination caused by previous land owners.

TRADE

Economic liberalisation (freer trade) will have a *generally positive* effect on the environment, by improving the efficient allocation of resources, by promoting economic growth and increasing general welfare, provided that effective environmental policies are implemented. OECD governments view trade liberalisation as a positive agent for change, which could provide new resources for environmental improvement, particularly in developing countries and countries in transition.

However, in the *absence* of effective environmental policies, including those aiming at internalising environmental costs, or when distortionary domestic policies exist, increased economic activity generated from trade liberalisation can contribute to environmental *problems*. The *net* environmental effects of liberalisation – both positive and negative – will therefore vary, depending on the country, sector and particular circumstances.

SECTORAL ECONOMIC ACTIVITIES

In the *energy* sector, for example, electricity deregulation has reduced incentives to use "dirty" fuels (or increased incentives to use "clean" ones) in some countries, but has led to the reverse pattern in others.

Increased competition in electricity production might also encourage suppliers to seek improvements in energy efficiency, reducing both emissions and the new investments in additional capacity that would otherwise have been required. On the other hand, increased competition might increase pressure for existing conservation-oriented environmental regulations to be eased.

Globalisation is likely to lower *transportation* prices across most modes, in most countries. Even where transportation prices rise in the short term (*e.g.* Central and Eastern Europe), the longer-term pressure on prices is likely to be downwards. Reduced prices, combined with the increased incomes that should result from a more efficient transport system generally, are likely to result in new demands for transport services. Increased demand for transport services may lead to new environmental stresses in the form of noise, air pollution, and congestion.

This *scale effect* has been exacerbated in recent years by *structural shifts* from the rail and shipping modes to road transport. In particular, much of the expansion in *freight* traffic that is being induced by globalisation is occurring on the road.

Some evidence suggests that the increased *economic* scale of global freight transport following trade liberalisation might not be very significant. On the other hand, the *environmental* effects of these changes could be quite significant. For one thing, "transit" countries may find that trade liberalisation *concentrates* freight traffic volumes on their networks. Thus, scale effects will have different environmental impacts in different countries, and those countries which already experience the highest impacts may suffer disproportionately from any increases in traffic volumes.

It is conceivable that positive environmental *technological and/or structural changes* in the freight sector might result from trade liberalisation. For example NAFTA is helping to reorient North American transport toward a more rational economic pattern (*e.g.* from an east-west axis, toward a north-south one). More open borders should allow shippers to use the most efficient routes to reach their markets, leading to *fewer* emissions and/or *reduced* energy consumption.

By inflating prices and farmer revenues, trade protectionism in the *agriculture sector* may be contributing both to increased *input use* and to the use of *monoculture technologies*, especially in OECD countries. At the same time, lower world prices may be depressing returns to developing country exports, thereby inhibiting key agriculture investments in those countries. One result can be the spread of low-yielding farming and ranching techniques into ecologically-vulnerable tropical forests. Trade liberalisation might *reduce* these environmental pressures. On the other hand, trade liberalisation might also cause the *scale* of agricultural production to expand, reinforcing any negative environmental externalities that current practices may be generating.

Similarly, reforming *agricultural support programmes* could alleviate some environmental problems and exacerbate others. The net environmental effects here will depend on the incentives actually provided to the farmer, on the physical characteristics of the land itself, on the specific crops/technologies being used, and on the policy context in which reforms are carried out.

The probability of achieving environmental improvements in the process of liberalising the agriculture sector can be enhanced if these reforms are accompanied by other policies which actually target environmental goals (*agri-environmental measures*). However, the design of these programmes needs to be carefully thought out, to prevent them from generating new environmental externalities and/or economic inefficiencies of their own.

TECHNOLOGY

By increasing the size of the market, globalisation provides firms with greater incentives to *innovate* (since they will realise even greater profits from successful innovations than would have been the case in the absence of trade). In addition, for those technological developments which require large production runs to be efficient, *diffusion rates* may increase. Globalisation-induced innovation based on increased competition also improves the chances that a firm will survive in a more globalised economic context, even where market size is *not* increasing.

New technologies developed for application in OECD countries may not be efficient when applied in developing country contexts. This may explain some of the observed differences in *diffusion rates* between OECD countries and LDCs. In extreme cases, it may also lead to "technology enclaves", in which advanced technology is transferred only to particular areas within LDCs.

Cost is a key determinant of whether or not a particular "clean" technology will be adopted. Although the *initial* cost of "process" technologies may sometimes be higher than that of "end-of-pipe" solutions, the former often generate *secondary* environmental and/or economic benefits for the firm. These secondary benefits are increasingly being recognised by industry, since there is a shift being observed towards "process" approaches in many OECD countries. This shift, coupled with the increasingly trans-frontier nature of business organisations, should lead to improvements in the environmental intensity of technology over the longer-term.

Influences on both the *supply* side (*e.g.* access to other factors of production) and the *demand* side (*e.g.* exposure to foreign consumption patterns) encourage the adoption of technologies with different environmental impacts. However, it is *not* certain *a priori* whether the combined effects of these two influences will be positive or negative for a particular sector, or in a particular country. For example, access to foreign technologies may displace existing domestic technologies which are better suited to local environmental conditions. On the other hand, it may allow firms to substitute *less*-damaging *foreign* equipment for *more*-damaging *domestic* machines.

The *environmental goods and services industry* is both a fast-growing and highly-traded sector in its own right. To the extent that economic globalisation promotes the international diffusion of output from this sector, it could have the effect of improving environmental conditions (or at least slowing down the rate of degradation).

The technology-globalisation-environment relationship needs to be reviewed at several *stages* (research, innovation, diffusion, and adoption). Each of these stages may produce different environmental results, and over different time horizons. However, a key challenge will clearly be to *reduce barriers to the diffusion and adoption* of appropriate new technologies, especially in the developing countries.

CORPORATE ENVIRONMENTAL STRATEGIES

The business community is likely to be in the "front line" of any environmental response to economic globalisation. Similarly, the way environmental and economic policies affect business behaviour will be an important determinant of business environmental strategies.

Much of the focus in globalisation-environment discussions centres around the role played by the Multi-National Enterprises (*MNEs*). MNEs are typically significant polluters and/or users of natural resources. They also maintain relatively high levels of R&D expenditure, and are capable of transferring pollution abatement technologies across international frontiers. They are also large – many now have annual outputs that exceed those of some developing countries.

On the other hand, the Small- and Medium-sized Enterprises (*SMEs*) are also generating a significant number of environmental problems. As these firms become more global in their outlooks, these problems may intensify. Special efforts therefore need to be made to understand the environmental needs, constraints, and opportunities associated with this group.

Much of the discussion about corporate environmental behaviour has centred around how to exploit "win-win" opportunities (*i.e.* where both corporate profits and environmental quality are enhanced). However, the real challenge for corporate environmentalism is *not* to persuade companies to pursue "win-win" strategies, but to deal with the more general case of achieving environmental goals, even at the *apparent* cost of reduced *short-term* profitability.

Globalisation is heightening the influence of *wider stakeholder interests* over the formulation of business strategies. These interests take the form of various pressures transmitted to the company from its "multiple stakeholder" groups, including regulators, consumers, insurers, trading partners, employees, and environmental non-governmental organisations.

FUTURE DIRECTIONS FOR THE OECD

The OECD is in an excellent position to provide some of the leadership currently lacking on globalisation-environment questions. Indeed, it is already moving in this direction in some areas (*e.g.* the ongoing negotiations toward a Multilateral Agreement on Investments are currently examining how environmental concerns might best be incorporated).

However, the *environmental* side of the globalisation-environment linkage needs to be more fully developed, and this is where the OECD could make a significant contribution to the debate. Two broad strategies are suggested:

- *Analyse* (both quantitatively and qualitatively) specific elements of the globalisation-environment relationship. *Quantitative empirical evidence* is currently lacking on virtually all components of this relationship. The amount of *environmental risk* associated with various globalisation scenarios, as well as the optimum levels of government response to these risks, should be a key part of any such analysis.

- Provide a *forum* and serve as a *catalyst* for *new co-operative international initiatives* aimed at reducing tensions in the globalisation-environment relationship (see the Governance Section for potential examples).

ECONOMIC GLOBALISATION
AND THE ENVIRONMENT

I. INTRODUCTION AND MAIN ISSUES

It is generally agreed that economic activity is becoming more "globalised". There is considerably less agreement about what this actually means in practice, or about whether globalisation will be a good or bad thing. But it does seem that the scale, structure, product mixes, and technological bases of economic activity are changing rapidly, and that these changes may have important implications for public policy.

This book explores these changes from one particular policy perspective – that of the environment. Its premise is that the globalisation process is altering the context of environmental problems at the local, national, regional, and global levels. In turn, this is generating new concerns about the generation and implementation of environmental policy. It is also opening up new opportunities to promote environmental objectives via the reorientation of economic policies.

Economic globalisation: key characteristics[1]

Globalisation can be thought of as a *process* in which economic markets, technologies, and communication patterns gradually exhibit more "global" characteristics, and less "national" or "local" ones. In this sense, it is the millions of daily decisions concerning technology choices, market structures/prices, and communication patterns that "drive" the globalisation process (see box). In altering these patterns, globalisation will generate a variety of consequences. These consequences will affect both the economy and the environment; they will also affect the global economy differently than they do that of individual nations.

Viewed at the world level, globalisation should enhance economic efficiency. This will allow world output to expand, in the form of additional economic growth (*scale effects*). It will also generate shifts in the composition and location of production and consumption activities (*structural effects*). More specifically, different technology paths will be promoted (*technology effects*), and different product mixes will be produced and consumed (*product effects*).

Economic globalisation – The driving forces

The rate of **technological change,** and how quickly new technology is diffused into the economy, are two basic elements of the globalisation process. It is often assumed that the rate of technological change and diffusion will increase as globalisation proceeds, thereby expanding production possibilities (and opportunities for economic growth).

Economic globalisation will also cause **market structures** to become both *deeper* (more geographic specialisation in production; more contracting-out to independent, but related, firms) and *wider* (more countries participating actively in the global economy).

- Seen from the perspective of *consumer* markets, globalisation might lead to more uniform consumer tastes, influenced by transnational mass media imagery and advertising.[2] Improvements in transportation and communication systems may also encourage some suppliers to locate their activities further away from their consumers.

- Seen from the perspective of *producer* markets, globalisation will be characterised by larger foreign investment flows, an increase in overseas commercial transactions (especially for primary and intermediate products), and a greater tendency to export final goods. Expansion may also be expected in the number and extent of international co-operative agreements between firms, notably in the fields of R&D, product supply, distribution, and marketing.[3] These arrangements will probably involve both inter- and intra-firm trades, and will almost certainly occur across international borders.

- Seen from the perspective of *individual firms*, globalisation will induce a myriad of new commercial relationships, which will in turn generate fundamental material and psychological changes, affecting the very core of business cultures.

Altered **communication patterns** are a third (highly-visible) characteristic of the globalisation process. As the OECD Council recently stated:

"Globalisation is both a cause and a consequence of the information revolution. It is driven by dramatic improvemen t of electronic communications networks, such as the Internet. These communications technologies are helping to overcome the barriers of physical distance. Communities of various types [...] now function across national borders. Even the framework of social policies affecting individual citizens is becoming more sensitive to international influences, including the global news media."[4]

Globalisation will not affect all of these parameters in the same way. For example, globalisation-induced *technology* changes may lead either to increases or to decreases in the *scale* of economic activity, depending on what types of technology are involved, the specific policy context in which these technologies are employed, and the relative substitutability/complementarity of the technologies being used in individual economies. It is the *net* effects of all changes together that will ultimately be of most interest, even though the individual (positive and negative) effects will also be of considerable interest in their own rights.

Economic *globalisation* is a different concept from that of economic *growth.* Globalisation *contributes to* economic growth, but is only one contributor. In particular, population growth, natural resource endowments, cultural heritage, etc., each play a role in the growth process. Each therefore also plays a role in determining how the scale, structure, technologies, and product mixes involved in global economic activity are ultimately determined.

However, the proportion of growth that can be attributed to globalisation is difficult to determine with certainty. Part of the reason for this uncertainty is that quantification inevitably depends on one's views about the "level of economic growth that would have occurred in the absence of globalisation". This *baseline issue* will complicate any "with/without" comparisons that may be attempted.

Although globalisation should improve the prospects for economic growth *world-wide*, it may also reduce economic prospects in *individual* countries, sectors, or industries. This will naturally be of concern to national governments in those countries where particular firms or industries might suffer economic declines as a result of globalisation. Thus, the way in which *competition and competitiveness* may be affected by globalisation will be of prime interest. At the national level, remaining competitive usually means attracting (and retaining) the business investments necessary to fuel economic growth (macro-competitiveness). At the level of the firm, it typically means providing a satisfactory return to shareholders (micro-competitiveness).

Globalisation will also reduce the ability of national governments to act unilaterally. Not only will the decisions of individual governments have less impact on the world economy, there will also be increased pressure on governments not to imperil the competitive position of their own constituents by taking unilateral action. Coupled with the globalisation-induced need for better regulatory frameworks to avert market failures, these tendencies all point to the need for the role of the nation state to evolve as globalisation proceeds. Thus, *institutional change* is likely to be another fundamental result of the globalisation process.

Competitiveness concerns, institutional reforms, and globalisation-induced changes in the structure and scale of economic activities, will be "played out" in three main areas of the economy: *i)* the international *trading* and *investment* systems; *ii)* specific *economic sectors*; and *iii)* individual *businesses*.

Life in the global economy will be full of uncertainty. Nowhere will this uncertainty be more politically troublesome than in the labour market, where disruptions in job security are already generating considerable debate about the effects of globalisation on *employment* prospects, and equally importantly, about the social costs and benefits of labour *migration*. On the other hand, globalisation is expected to generate additional growth in the world economy, suggesting that globalisation may generate *positive* employment effects overall.

A key mechanism through which globalisation will achieve the economic benefits it promises is the *liberalisation of economic activity*. The signing of the Marrakech Agreement testified to the broad emphasis now being given to achieving lower tariffs in world trade. Discussions are also under way within the OECD aimed at reaching a Multilateral Agreement on Investments – an accord which would reduce barriers to the international flow of investment. Economic liberalisation can also manifest itself as a higher ratio of private sector involvement in economic activity (*i.e.* privatisation), or in fewer regulations (*i.e.* deregulation).

Equity issues

In theory, globalisation should lead to a more efficient allocation of scarce economic resources, but it may also generate social tensions in the process, as these changes begin to affect specific individuals or groups. Those affected will often perceive the costs of these changes more readily than they do the benefits. To use a current example, local employment problems are often blamed on freer trade, which rarely gets any of the credit for new employment opportunities generated elsewhere in the economy. Theory suggests that some of the savings from increased economic efficiency could be redirected towards social goals, to everyone's advantage. In practice, however, these reallocations may be difficult to achieve.

There are two broad types of equity-based tensions that will probably result from the globalisation process: *inter*-generational and *intra*-generational. The former relate to the concern that today's pollution/resource use will simply transfer environmental problems onto future generations. The latter tensions relate to the distribution of environmental impacts and the costs of avoiding these impacts within the current generation. Although both types are of concern, it is intra-generational problems which are generating much of the public debate about the merits and demerits of globalisation.

The increased mobility of certain factors of production (especially capital, but also labour) is generating much of the concern among those opposed to globalisation. For example, it has been observed[5] that "at the beginning of the 1970s, 90% of foreign exchange transactions financed trade and long-term investment; only 10% were speculative. Today, the opposite is true, with the increased speculation translating into considerable labour market uncertainties, volatile currency exchange rates, and other undesirable results. Little account has been taken by the champions of flexible labour markets of these high social costs. ... In effect, this adds up to a picture of stress in work and stress out of work – a deeply unhealthy social picture."

Some observers are even blunter: "GATT, [like] the theories on which it is based, is flawed. If it is implemented, it will impoverish and destabilise the industrialised world, while at the same time cruelly ravaging the third world."[6]

It is not surprising that the OECD, as one of the world's foremost proponents of economic liberalisation, should be associated with the more optimistic view of globalisation.[7] For example, the OECD Council recently stated:

"The globalisation of the economy ... gives all countries the possibility of participating in world development, and all consumers the assurances of bene-fiting from increasingly vigorous competition between producers. To take advantage of these prospects for improved living conditions and progress, individuals, enterprises, and countries must show themselves capable of rapid adjustment and continuous innovation. This is the challenge, particularly for Member countries."[8]

Note that this conclusion is phrased in the conditional. Countries have the *potential* to derive significant benefits from the globalisation process, but there is still the problem of *realising* this potential. What might prevent its realisation? Mainly, it is the possibility that too much attention will be paid to economic goals (such as efficiency), and not enough to broader social ones (such as equity).

Globalisation and environment: main issues

The framework developed above for linking globalisation with its *economic* consequences can also serve to analyse the relationship between globalisation and its *environmental* consequences. Thus, in contributing to economic growth, global-isation will also affect the environment in many of the same ways that economic growth does (see box).

This also implies that globalisation will have impacts on progress toward the broader goal of *sustainable development*, but globalisation will again be only one of the determinants of progress toward this goal.

The scale, technology, structural, and product effects discussed earlier will each also generate environmental consequences. Competitiveness concerns will arise in the implementation of *environmental* policies, just as they do for the implementa-tion of *economic* policies. The role of the nation state in the creation and imple-mentation of environmental policies will need to evolve, just as it needs to evolve in the economic policy field. All of these environmental consequences may be either positive or negative, and again, it will be the *net* environmental effects that will ultimately be of most interest.

Economic globalisation is not equivalent to the globalisation of environmental problems, such as climate change. Obviously, these *can* be related (*e.g.* where more intense global economic activity leads to an increase in greenhouse gas emissions). But the environmental effects of economic globalisation are not *limited* to global environmental issues: it is the entire range of environmental impacts of globalisa-tion that are considered here – *i.e.* impacts at the local, national, regional and global levels.

Analysing the environmental consequences of globalisation must be done over a longer time frame than is required for many economic issues. Some elements of a more globalised economy may *initially* seem benign (or even positive) for the

Key environment-economy relationships

An efficient economy *requires* that environmental costs be taken into account when economic decisions are made. An efficient economy also produces the maximum possible level of resources with which to fight environmental degradation. Thus, even though environmental policy may sometimes seem opposed to economic objectives, it may only be economic *growth* (at least as traditionally measured) that is being affected, while still contributing to economic *welfare*.

Environmental policy is often seen as having a negative impact on social equity, since the poorest groups tend to bear the largest relative burden of these policies. But the poorest groups also already bear a disproportionate share of the harm that pollution causes, so it is not clear that they will always be worse off *with* effective environmental policies than they are *without* them.

Social cohesion may be impaired by a lack of adequate environmental policies. Access to a healthy, clean environment is now firmly rooted in social expectations.

A key environment-economy challenge will be to decide what the "right" level of environmental protection will be. This depends on the values people are willing to place on present and future environmental protection. Although there is considerable uncertainty surrounding these values, a few general conclusions can be drawn from theory:

- The "right" level of environmental protection will vary by country; different local circumstances will lead to different values being placed on environmental protection.

- Most countries will prefer higher levels of environmental quality, the higher their income levels.

- The worse environmental quality becomes, the more the costs of further environmental degradation will increase.

- The further economic integration proceeds, the more likely it is that common views about environmental problems will emerge; thus, opportunities for collective action will increase.

- It is reasonably certain that the "right" level of environmental protection is higher than current levels, mainly because the risks of long-term, irreversible environmental damage are typically ignored in present-day economic decision-making.

environment, but may seem quite the opposite when viewed in a *more dynamic (i.e.* longer-term) way. It may also be that the rate of globalisation is not constant over time; similarly, the rate of *environmental* change due to globalisation may not be constant. A dynamic and long-term approach to analysing these environmental effects is therefore required.

There is considerable uncertainty about the long-term ability of the environment to withstand the pressures of even the current scale of economic activity, let alone the scale that might exist after the world economy has become more globalised. Globalisation may therefore place significant new stresses on environmental resources, unless new measures are put in place to avert this result.

On the other hand, globalisation may open up opportunities for structural and/or technological changes that offset these scale effects in certain situations. This would imply that the (negative) scale effects of globalisation on the environment might be held to lower levels over time than the (positive) technological and structural effects.

However, betting on this possibility will be quite risky from an environmental perspective. The main source of this risk is that the long-term environmental consequences of today's economic behaviour are poorly understood. This implies that the long-term environmental effects of globalisation cannot be viewed strictly through the lens of today's economic interests. A "precautionary approach" is therefore required, to account for the possibility that current perceptions about future environmental conditions may turn out to be wrong (and perhaps, *very* wrong). On the other hand, the actual level of "precaution" to be applied, as well as the particular instruments to be used in implementing this approach, both need to be clearly thought out.

Unfortunately, it is much easier to support the "precautionary approach" in principle than it is in practice. This is partly because policy decisions tend to be based on *current realities*, not on *future possibilities*. It is also partly because most analytical tools available for the analysis of economic/environmental processes focus largely on the short- and medium-terms, leaving aside longer-term considerations.

Technological change and the changed structure of economic markets are generating three broad trends of fundamental interest to the environment.[9] First, there is the trend away from environmentally-intensive outputs and/or factors of production. For example, services make up an increasing share of GDP in industrialised countries; on the other hand, some developing countries are experiencing a shift from agriculture to heavy industry. Capital and knowledge are increasingly the sources of economic prosperity, to the detriment of two other key factors – labour and raw materials. The net result may be that the era of mass production is giving way to a new age – one in which electronics and information will dominate.

The second trend is towards a certain "dematerialisation" of economic activity. For example, each unit of GDP is now being produced with fewer inputs of some environmental resources. This is especially true in the energy sector, where combustion efficiencies improved significantly in some countries after the oil price increases of the 1970s. On the other hand, wastage of many natural resources continues, often driven by implicit or explicit subsidies that encourage over-production or over-use. Water resources are an often-cited example of this latter problem.

A third perceived trend is sometimes referred to as "depollution" – the idea that levels of pollution per unit of GDP are falling, and that pollution is being "decoupled" from economic production. An example comes from the transport sector: modern automobiles produce much less pollution per unit than their predecessors, mainly because of catalytic converters. Much of the progress towards depollution is being fuelled by improvements in the technologies underlying eco nomic growth. Thus, technological development will often provide the main ways o reducing the negative effects of globalisation on the environment (or increasing th benefits).

Although these positive trends are likely to be reinforced by the globalisatio process, the full story may not be quite so optimistic. For one thing, the negativ *scale* effects of globalisation may turn out to be very large, effectively swamping an positive technological and/or structural effects. Despite encouraging reductions i the *average* intensities of pollution loads and resource usage, the *total* burden o the environment may be higher in a more globalised economic context than it i today.

For another thing, depollution and dematerialisation are being observed pr marily in the developed countries. Many developing countries (especially th rapidly-developing ones) are not yet showing such patterns. Both the large popula tions and rapid economic growth rates in developing countries suggest that th relative shares of some pollution loads in world totals are shifting towards cour tries where environmental controls are not always as high as they are in OEC countries.

Some observers[10] have also argued that at least some forms of pollutio exhibit inverted-U (*i.e.* Kuznets) relationships with economic development ove time. In this view, although industrialisation and agricultural modernisation ma initially lead to increased pollution as growth increases, other factors may cause a eventual downturn, at least for some pollutants.

Because developing countries are at an earlier stage in the development pro cess, it might therefore be "natural" for their economies to exhibit more pollutior intensive characteristics than the industrialised countries do. Therefore, the *move ment* of pollution-intensive activities from the OECD to the developing countrie might not be cause for special concern. On the other hand, the level of income a which developing country pollution begins to improve may be quite a bit highe than current levels. In any event, the influence of incomes on pollution may also nc turn out to be as strong as first thought.

Finally, if countries move their pollution-intensive *production* to other cour tries, but maintain their existing *consumption* practices, their relative responsibilit for world-wide pollution has probably not really declined. Because most enviror mental statistics account for pollution on a production basis (rather than on consumption basis), the way in which responsibility for pollution/resource over-us problems is usually perceived may not be totally accurate.

In the following sections, some of the most important components of th globalisation-environment linkage are further explored, largely from the perspe tives of how economic liberalisation might affect each linkage (see box). In thinking about each of these issues, two basic points should be kept in mind:

- All empirical results presented in this book are based on specific assumptions made by individual researchers, and for their particular contexts. It is therefore often very difficult to extrapolate these results to other countries, problems, or situations more generally.

- The various environmental effects of globalisation (technology, scale, structural, product, and regulatory) are not mutually exclusive. They will therefore tend to overlap each other (in a quantitative sense), and "double-counting" of effects may become a problem.

Globalisation and environment – Summary of main issues

- **Governance.** Largely because of competitiveness problems, governments will probably find their scope for unilateral action somewhat reduced in a more globalised economy. To achieve their environmental objectives, governments may have to resort more often to collective action at the international level. However, international action to resolve environmental issues is still in its infancy, so progress in this direction may be slow.

- **Competitiveness.** Competitiveness issues lie at the core of the globalisation-environment relationship. Some see competitiveness concerns leading to a "lowest common denominator" approach to environmental policy.[11] In this view, globalisation will generate pressure to reduce the impact of environmental policies on domestic firms. Globalisation would therefore represent a direct *threat* to the environment. On the other hand, globalisation may be an *opportunity* for the environment, to the extent that effective environmental policies are seen as a way of enhancing national competitiveness and/or encouraging the efficient use of resources.

- **Technology.** Technological change represents an important opportunity for reducing the negative environmental effects of the globalisation process. This opportunity needs to be reviewed at several stages (research, innovation, diffusion, and adoption). Each of these stages may produce different environmental results, and over different time horizons. On the other hand, technological change also involves environmental risks (*e.g.* contributing to the increased *scale* of economic output).

- **Trade and investment.** International trade and investment are highly-visible parts of the economic globalisation process. Although they are not "anti-environmental" in their own right, they are often accused of contributing to environmental degradation, especially where effective environmental controls are lacking. On the other hand, trade and investment policies are powerful economic levers which might contribute to the achievement of environmental goals within the globalisation context.

- **Sectoral economic activities.** Globalisation may generate pressure to reform the pricing systems (subsidies and taxes) which exist in the environmentally-important energy, transport and agriculture sectors. Trade liberalisation, deregulation, and privatisation may also change the context in which these activities occur, generating both favourable and unfavourable environmental impacts along the way.

- **Business strategies.** The business community (especially multinational enterprises) is likely to be in the front line of any environmental response to economic globalisation. Similarly, the way environmental and economic policies affect business behaviour will be an important determinant of business environmental strategies.

2. GOVERNANCE[12]

Market-based policy convergence in the global economy

Market-driven economic globalisation creates pressures for economic *performance* in different countries to become more alike. Of course, market integration wi[ll] never be perfect, even among the (relatively homogeneous) OECD countries. However, some empirical studies[13] *do* find evidence of some economic convergence both within and between broad categories of "rich" and "poor" countries.

Integration in economic *performance* then "drives" a process leading towar[d] convergence in economic *policies*. The deeper and broader the level of marke[t] integration, the greater this policy convergence will be. In addition, the larger th[e] national market share of a given country in global trade and capital flows, th[e] greater the forces of convergence will be toward the economic policies of tha[t] nation. At the global level, the OECD countries are simultaneously the "large[ ] market" countries, and the most highly integrated. Economic policy convergence i[s] therefore likely both within the OECD group, as well as from the developing countries toward the OECD.

Convergence is especially likely in the area of macroeconomic policies. Indeed broad international agreement on more "open" trade and investment policies i[s] itself a prerequisite for globalisation. But OECD governments are also typicall[y] constrained to keep key elements of their *domestic* macroeconomic policies (e.[g.] interest rates) within "similar" bands.

The forces leading to *economic* policy convergence also work in the direction o[f] *environmental* policy convergence. Although there are few empirical studies suggesting that the imposition of higher environmental costs on one's own firms wi[ll] *actually* reduce their competitiveness (see Section 3), there is often a *perceptio[n]* that this result will occur. This perception is then often used as a justification for [a] given country's environmental policies to converge toward those of its primar[y] competitors.

Convergence in environmental *product standards* is also driven by nationa[l] policies. This is especially true for import requirements imposed by large-marke[t] countries. The larger the import market, the greater the impact of domestic standards on international standards. On the other hand, *production and proces[s] methods* are less subject to policy convergence, partly because WTO rules hav[e] discouraged countries from unilaterally imposing this type of standard on import[s.]

Environmental policy convergence is likely to be most pronounced amon[g] countries whose markets are the most highly integrated, as well as among countrie[s] which are the most homogenous in economic capacity. Among *rich countries*, som[e] environmental product and production standards are therefore likely to converg[e] round an "OECD average", as well as around industry-wide averages (in the case of internationally-exposed industries).

The primary export markets for *developing countries* are the OECD countries. Developing country product standards are therefore generally pulled toward the OECD average, as their export markets become more deeply and more broadly integrated with the OECD. On the other hand, the primary competition for developing countries as "production platforms" comes from other developing countries. In this specific case, developing country product standards are likely to converge not towards the OECD level, but towards some developing country benchmark. Later, as the sectoral composition of their production gradually becomes more like that of the OECD countries, developing country environmental product standards are then likely to move in the direction of the OECD average.

This implies that what the OECD group does to address the environmental problems associated with globalisation will matter a lot. In this regard, *OECD leadership"* will be critical. It also suggests that the policy reaction of an individual OECD country to the environmental consequences of globalisation is likely to be "conditioned" *mostly* by policies adopted by its major trading partners (generally, the other OECD countries), rather than in the developing ones. (It is true that some developing countries are growing rapidly, and will therefore probably be the sources of some important new environmental stresses in the future. However, the faster these economies grow, the more likely their environmental policies are to converge with those of the OECD group in any event.)

OECD environmental policy innovations may therefore be constrained by the need to obtain agreement among its major trading partners ("prisoner's dilemma"). In the absence of such agreement, environmental policy innovations may tend to converge around the *status quo*. Unfortunately, the *status quo* may not be enough to address the full range of environmental problems that could be associated with globalisation.

Market-driven policy convergence will therefore *reduce* competitiveness problems, but will not *eliminate* them. Competitiveness issues will still "condition" the required environmental policy response. In addition, market-based policy responses might not even be sufficient to address the *ecological* bases of globalisation environment problems. This is because:

- Markets often do not capture environmental externalities at all.
- Even where they do capture these externalities, markets are typically not sensitive to local ecological conditions. In effect, markets work in the direction of *convergence*, whereas efficiency in the design/delivery of environmental policies requires *diversity*, to reflect variations in *local* conditions.
- Countries have even less reason to use markets as a vehicle for internalising transfrontier/global externalities than they do for internalising *domestic*

ones. In a globalising economy, more environmental problems are likely to become transboundary in nature.

International co-operation

For all these reasons, policy intervention by governments will continue to b necessary as globalisation proceeds. The precise form that this intervention shoul take will depend on the particular circumstances at hand. From the perspective c economic efficiency, any such intervention should be made at the same level as th externality itself – thus, local externalities should be addressed by local response global ones should be addressed at the global level. (Of course, other policy goal besides economic efficiency, such as *environmental effectiveness* or *distributiv issues*, are often at stake, and could alter this principle in certain situations.)

In a more globalised economy, the boundaries between *environmental* effect (externalities) and *economic* effects (especially competitiveness problems) wi become less distinct. In addition, local environmental effects will increasingly hav international economic consequences, and global environmental problems can gen erate local economic impacts. This implies that there may be no such thing as truly "national" environmental externality.

If this is so, at least three types of government intervention may be warrantec *i)* national policies to internalise the environmental costs of those domestic exter nalities which have *no* international competitiveness implications; *ii)* co-operativ arrangements with other governments to address those domestic environmenta externalities which do have international competitiveness implications; and *iii)* co operative arrangements with other governments for addressing transfrontier/globa environmental externalities.

The first case involves only national policies, and is not dealt with further here The latter two cases imply some form of multilateral co-operation aimed at resolv ing environmental problems. This co-operation would have several defining charac teristics: *i)* it would not necessarily target international environmental externalitie it could also cover domestic externalities where significant international competi tiveness concerns exist; *ii)* it would not only involve *environmental* interests indeed, the reasons for the co-operation in the first place would often be related t competitiveness (*i.e. economic*) problems, more than environmental ones; *iii)* i would not necessarily involve *all countries*. Many environmental (and competitive ness) problems have more relevance at the regional scale than they do at the globa level. Even in the particular case of *global* environmental issues, international co operation might be more efficient if it were organised at the sub-global level, give the significant transaction costs that can be associated with involving a large number of countries.

International co-operation of the type suggested here could take various forms e.g. voluntary actions, codes of conduct, guidelines, formal agreements, etc.). A few areas in which any or all of these different forms might be considered for future initiatives by the OECD include:

First, new opportunities may exist for reducing globalisation-induced *environmental* problems in the context of regional *economic* groupings. The Asia Pacific Economic Co-operation (APEC) forum provides one (but not the only) possible model. APEC encompasses a relatively small group of both developing and developed countries. It was also formed with a loose mandate to provide trade and investment liberalisation elements of globalisation; and it has embraced environmental, technical, and development co-operation within its agenda.

APEC initiatives are based on "concerted unilateralism:" Broad regional goals of common interest are defined, the specific aspects of which are implemented nationally. Neither side payments nor the threat of economic sanctions are emphasised, thereby reducing some of the political opposition to change from both developed and developing countries. Instead, the focus is on a perception of mutual self-interest, as well as on more subtle forms of longer-term political pressure.

This consensus-building approach has been important in gaining regional support for an environmental agenda. It may also increase the likelihood that any initiatives taken at the regional level will actually be implemented at the national one. However, the "APEC Model" also has its limitations. The need for consensus means that controversial issues can sometimes be avoided. A lack of institutional transparency and formal participatory mechanisms can also sometimes inhibit accountability and public input.

Second, opportunities probably exist for improved integration of the competitiveness/financial and environmental objectives of key international organisations. In particular, it will be important to ensure that international financial/economic institutions (*e.g.* World Bank, EBRD, IADB) and *trade* organisations (*e.g.* WTO) take account of environmental concerns, and that international environmental organisations (*e.g.* UNEP) take explicit account of competitiveness concerns in their respective efforts.

Third, the voluntary "community partnership" approach might be further developed at the international level. This approach would build on the common interests of governments, the international business community, and community groups with international interests. It would also involve an explicit recognition that domestic environmental problems, as well as generating international competitiveness concerns. Involving businesses and local communities directly in improving *world-wide* environmental performance is likely to yield faster and broader results than relying on governments alone.

One way of doing this might be to envisage *voluntary action plans* on key environmental issues of interest to both business and governments. For example, the Japanese Government has recently taken two such initiatives related risk management. Action plans were first developed by the Japanese Chemical Industries Association (through MITI), and then submitted to the OECD for formal recognition. A similar model could be envisaged for other types of environmental problems involving a wider range of business interests. Two globalisation-related priorities of this type might include:

- A larger role for the business sector (and indeed, the general public) in *monitoring and compliance* activities.
- Special efforts need to be made to understand the environmental needs, constraints, and opportunities associated with the SMEs (see Section 8).

Fourth, opportunities may exist for improving the ability of the developing countries to adopt and absorb new *technologies*, as well as to set in place the institutional capability to foster environmentally-friendly innovations themselves ("capacity-building").

Fifth, A whole new set of statistics, basic data, and indicators are likely to be needed in the future at the *global* level to complement existing data and information initiatives at the national level (*e.g.* productivity data which accounts for environmental factors; "green accounts" at the global level, etc.). More specific opportunities could be explored in the following areas:

- Data to evaluate the environmental externalities in *producer* countries of *consumption* patterns in another country.
- Data on *environmental* sectors, rather than just on *economic* ones (*e.g.* accounts of international flows of selected natural resources or materials).
- The application of indicators of environmental performance to global and/or international issues (*e.g.* degree of achievement of international commitments).

3. COMPETITIVENESS[14]

The political focus on competitiveness has grown to such an extent that new policies are often effectively subjected to a "competitiveness test". For example, opponents of trade liberalisation typically argue that open markets will damage the competitiveness of some economies because of increased competition from lower cost economies.

When examining the relationship between competitiveness and the environment, it is useful to differentiate the effects at the level of the individual *firm* from those at the broader (*i.e.* general equilibrium) level of industries and the national economy in general. Competitiveness will also raise quite different problems in the short-term (*static effects*) than they do in the long-term (*dynamic effects*).

Perspective of the firm

For an individual firm, competitiveness means the ability to sell goods or services in the market-place, and to stay in business. Loss of competitiveness could be manifested by loss of sales, loss of market share, and ultimately, by plant closures. But do increased environmental costs imposed on firms necessarily translate into a loss of competitiveness? There are at least five reasons why this may not be so:

- It is primarily the cost differential *between* firms that gives rise to the competitiveness effect. If all competing firms face the same cost increase, then amongst themselves, there will *not* be a relative shift in costs and prices, or any change in competitiveness.

- The degree to which any new costs impact on sales will depend on: *i)* whether these costs can be passed on to consumers; *ii)* the price response of competitors; and *iii)* the price-sensitivity of the demand for the product. For example, increased environmental costs will translate into greater effects on the competitiveness of a firm, the more narrow its profit margin: the greater the degree of competition in a market, and the more price-elastic the demand for the good or service.

- Firms do not operate in a *static* environment. Facing increased costs, firms will have an incentive to adapt their operations, in order to reduce the impact of that increase. This will set in motion a whole host of measures aimed at "neutralising" the original cost increase. Technological development, improved environmental management and factor substitution are three potential responses of this type.

- Environmental policy is only one of a vast array of factors that will determine the overall competitiveness of a firm. Management ability, the capacity to innovate; patterns of world supply and demand; and proximity to raw materials and important markets, are only a few of the other factors involved.

- The ability to provide what the consumer wants is the ultimate competitive survival strategy for a firm. If consumers demand improved environmental performance from firms, it could mean that improved environmental performance is a *precondition for*, not a *detractor from*, firm competitiveness.

The traditional hypothesis is that higher environmental standards cause business costs to increase, thereby *reducing* both profits and competitiveness. The countervailing hypothesis is that better environmental performance actually reduces costs and/or improves product quality, thereby *improving* firm competitiveness, especially over the long-term.

One recent study,[15] covering about 2 000 firms from a wide range of narrowly-specified industries, concluded that there is no overall tendency for plants with superior environmental performance to be less profitable. It was also concluded that plants with lower emissions (relative to production) actually achieve *higher* operating margins and returns on invested capital. However, it was observed that both of these correlations were relatively weak.

Another study[16] of 67 firms in the dairy and meat processing industries in Europe concluded that:

- Firms can achieve high levels of competitiveness, even with relatively high regulatory costs.
- There was no clear evidence that firms with above-average productivities also had relatively low compliance costs.
- Environmental costs were *not* one of the important factors influencing the survival (or the growth) of most firms.
- There was a generally *positive* association between above-average levels of competitiveness and above-average adoption of environmental initiatives.

An ethic of eco-efficiency, or "clean" production, which seeks to avoid pollution problems in the first place, rather than deal with unwanted waste streams later, is an increasingly accepted business perspective. Viewed as a resource efficiency issue, minimising the environmental impact of production *ex ante* is more likely to yield cost-reducing or quality-enhancing outcomes, compared with *ex post* "end-of-pipe" solutions. A "resource efficiency" perspective sees waste discharges as an inefficient use of raw materials. Eliminating this inefficiency, at least up to a certain point, can therefore be a good way of *increasing* competitiveness.

Perspective of industry

One company's loss in profitability may be a gain to another competitor in the same industry. An industry is the aggregation of all firms which are exploiting similar economic activities, but the precise composition of this aggregate will vary as the fortunes of individual firms rise and fall. At the industry level, "competitiveness" is often thought to derive from having to face lower costs than international rivals in the same industry.

It is worth recalling here that the objective of environmental policy is often to *reduce* either the use of inputs (*e.g.* energy) or the production of outputs (*e.g.* emissions) which harm the environment. These changes are often closely linked to the competitiveness of an industry (via the industry's cost structure). Thus, the "real" debate should often be *not* about the loss of industrial or national competitiveness, but about whether or not the environmental policy itself will produce a benefit to society.

Many studies examine how environmental policy will affect economic activity through industry level statistics, such as *productivity* (the efficiency with which inputs are translated into outputs). However, a key problem with productivity measures is that environmental expenditures are counted as *inputs*, but they are not counted as contributing to the *output* being measured (*i.e.* the product sold on the market). This is because they "only" serve to avoid environmental harms. Thus, environmental policies will decrease productivity *by definition*.

There are also several "real" ways in which environmental policies might affect productivity, both negatively and positively. On the negative side, pollution control equipment might reduce the engineering efficiency of production processes. On the positive side, environment policies could speed up the search for new production processes that have increased technical efficiencies.

In one study that examined plant-level data for the paper, oil refining, and steel industries for the 1979-1990 period, it was found that plants with higher abatement costs did indeed have significantly lower productivity levels.[17] However, this result applied only to variations *across* plants. Estimates looking at productivity variations *within* plants showed a smaller (and insignificant) relationship between abatement costs and productivity. In addition, other measures of environmental regulations faced by the plants (compliance status, enforcement activity) were *not* significantly related to productivity.

Since these results hold only for *levels* (and not *rates*) of change, and since a link was found only *across* plants (not *within* one plant over time), a plausible interpretation is that there are simply "good" and "bad" plants. Good plants are more productive, more likely to comply with regulations, and better at finding low-cost means of compliance. Low productivity and high enforcement costs may both be caused by a third factor – poor management. This interpretation is consistent with other recent studies on firm innovation and environmental performance.

A recent US study of productivity changes in the 1970s concluded that 8-16% of all reductions in factor productivity were due to environmental regulation.[18] Larger reductions were attributed to environmental policy in specific sectors (*e.g.* 10% for the chemical industry; 30% for paper producers; 44% for electric utilities).

However, all of these studies have the problem of the "measurement effect", described earlier. Researchers have therefore been looking for new ways of calculating productivity, in order to reduce this bias. One recent study even attempted to introduce environmental improvements (*i.e.* reduced environmental damages) into the calculation for three environmentally-sensitive industries. Not surprisingly, the inclusion of environmental damages changes the results considerably (see Table 1),

Table 1.   **Revising productivity measures to include environmental outputs**

Sector	Period	Multifactor productivity (average annual % change)		
		Conventional MFP	Revised MFP (constant damage values)	Revised MFP (damage values proportional to GDP)
Electricity	1970-91	−0.35	0.68	0.38
Pulp and paper	1970-90	0.16	0.44	0.36
Agriculture	1977-92	2.30	2.41	2.38

Source: Repetto et al. (1996), Table 1.2.

but will probably lead to considerable debate about the values that this study placed on these environmental damages.

While an increase in the stringency of environmental regulation will affect the comparative advantage of an industry within the *domestic* economy, the extent to which it affects its competitive advantage in *world* markets depends on its response in comparison with the response of foreign rival industries.

A series of comparative industry studies have recently been carried out in the US, looking at the competitive implications of environmental regulations in different circumstances.[19] Overall, these studies confirm that the rate of industrial innovation depends on both the nature of the environmental regulations and the particular structure of the industry. In some cases, the industry in the country which was *first* exposed to a new regulation gained a "first-mover" advantage. In other cases, a *delayed* response yielded higher competitive advantages. The use of "transition strategies" also generally proved to be beneficial.

National competitiveness

There is no straightforward relationship between competitiveness at the firm industry levels with "competitiveness" at the national level. In a dynamic economy there will always be firms and industries which are growing, and those which are declining. Plant closures and local unemployment are very painful for those affected, and are also highly visible in political terms. However, national economies are absorbing this type of structural adjustment all the time, to accommodate changes in technologies, consumer tastes, and general demand/supply conditions. Changes in environmental policy generally play only a very small part in these shifts.

From an environmental perspective, making polluters pay for the pollution they generate has the effect of *reducing* the comparative advantage of polluting industries. By definition, therefore, non-polluting industries will find that their comparative advantage has *increased*. In addition, reduced industrial emissions will mean that some industries will face lower costs from having fewer environmental damages imposed on them. It is the net economic effect of all these forces which should be considered at the national level, not the effect on any single firm or industry.

Those concerned about competitiveness would predict that an increase in regulatory stringency would lead to a fall in the *net exports* of heavily regulated sectors, relative to the net exports of less regulated sectors. Some researchers do find such a negative correlation,[20] but others do not.[21] Even where a negative relationship *is* found, however, it tends to be stronger when the study focuses only on the *exports* of pollution-intensive industries, and when the level of aggregation of the analysis is at or near the level of *specific products*. When the analysis moves to *higher* levels of aggregation, or when the focus is on *imports*, the relationship either becomes quite small, or actually changes sign. Both of these latter results are counter-intuitive to the original hypothesis.

The pollution-intensity of *specific trade flows* has also been examined from this perspective, with largely similar results. Looking at overall world trade patterns, for example, one recent study[22] found that the share of industrial country *imports* of environmentally-sensitive goods originating in developing countries rose only slightly between 1970 and 1990. In effect, the data suggests that OECD countries are maintaining their share of pollution-intensive trade overall, despite the raising of environmental standards throughout most of the OECD Region during this period.

Although pollution intensive trade flows in *individual* countries *have* undergone significant structural changes between 1970 and 1990, these shifts were clearly due to much larger forces than just environmental compliance costs. In particular, the *structural shifts* toward services in the OECD countries, and toward industry in the developing ones, seem to have been more important than changes in environmental policies themselves. For example, Finland and Austria maintain relatively high environmental standards *and* a high share of environmentally-sensitive goods in their export compositions, but both countries were nevertheless able to increase or maintain their world shares of manufacturing exports over the twenty years of this study.

The share of environmentally-sensitive goods in *total exports* is also quite variable across OECD countries, but has generally fallen in all countries. Again, this is not because of changes in environmental standards, but because of structural shifts in other sectors (*e.g.* Norway's share fell as a result of increased oil exports). On balance, there has *not* been any significant decline in the market shares of environmentally-sensitive goods in those countries which have higher environmental standards.

At a more disaggregated level, however, the same study found that the industrial countries *did* lose some revealed comparative advantage in most of the pollution-intensive product categories that were analysed, at the same time as the developing countries were increasing their shares in these particular products. Once again, however, these shifts are largely due to structural conditions, rather than to environmental ones. For example, the increased comparative advantage of the developing countries in iron and steel reflects both the increased role of the developing countries in world trade and the fact that heavy industries are typically prominent in the early stages of the development process (see also Sections **1** and 6).

The data is not very clear at the national level either. For example, Germany (a relatively high-standard country) has maintained its revealed comparative advantage in the chemicals and metals industries, both of which have the highest environmental compliance costs within the manufacturing sector. On the other hand Germany has *lost* some revealed comparative advantage in other product areas which are *less* environmentally-sensitive.

International competitiveness

Part of the confusion surrounding the environment/competitiveness debate relates to the fact that countries do not compete with each other in the same way that firms do. While their firms' products compete with each other as rivals, trading nations are not so much "competitors" as they are each other's customers and suppliers. Talking about Country A's competitiveness (often defined in terms of *trade* performance), relative to Country B's, implies that countries compete only as *producers* of goods and services. But countries are both producers and consumers and consumers will benefit from having better access to imported products. The pre-occupation with competitiveness probably reflects the fact that producer interests often dominate over consumer interests in establishing trade policies. But trade is *not* a "zero-sum game" – both exporter and importer countries benefit from it.

One important conclusion from this is that trade balances at the macroeconomic level *cannot* be taken as simple measures of national competitiveness. The single most important reflection of a nation's international competitiveness in the short term is probably its exchange rate, which is in itself determined by a highly complex set of economic factors. Many commentators also argue that it is *productivity growth* which is the best measurable indicator of competitiveness in the longer-term (see above). However, productivity growth usually means an increase in output per unit of input within the domestic economy (*i.e.* not relative to other countries). One country's improved productivity does not come at the "expense" of reduced productivity in another country.

This is not to say that governments do not compete to maintain and attract investment and the resultant employment in their territories. Computing, telecommunications, modern transport and lower trade barriers, tax policy differentiation (*i.e.* forces all associated with "globalisation") mean that producers have greater freedom to choose where they will locate their operations. Each of these elements stimulates competition, and ultimately gives producer interests political leverage for resisting new policies which might increase their business costs.

The overall objective of *environmental* policy is *not* to promote the international competitiveness of industry — it is to promote sustainable development. Environmental policy will increase social welfare if the overall benefits it generates are greater than the costs. The pertinent question is therefore whether the environmental measure is worth the cost to the overall society, not whether a particular firm or industry suffers.

The application of a social cost/benefit test, the adoption of the most efficient regulatory regime, and transition policies can each be applied more easily to domestic environmental issues than they can to international ones. Globalisation increases economic interconnections across borders, meaning that policy-makers have to deal with "leakage" in both an economic and an environmental sense. If a *national* environmental policy aimed at an *international* problem eventually results in industrial relocation, with no reduction in global environmental damage, it is clearly ineffective in both environmental and economic terms.

4. FOREIGN INVESTMENT[23]

Discussion about global private capital flows often centres on *foreign direct investment* (FDI). Although FDI is an important source of *private international finance* (PIF), it represented only 54% of the total PIF flows to emerging markets in 1995.[24] *Debt finance* contributed a further 33%, and *portfolio investments* the remaining 13%. Each of these sources varies in its relationship with environmental problems. Although FDI gets most of the attention in that relationship, the other two types are growing fast, and will have to receive more emphasis in the future as to their environmental consequences.

Despite a slight decline in ODA, developing countries are currently receiving new capital flows far in excess of anything thought possible just a few years ago (Figure 1). Most of these flows are originating in private markets, rather than from governments.

Nearly 75% of the flow of PIF in recent years has actually gone to OECD countries.[25] Similarly, the vast majority of funds made available overseas through equity investments still go to companies based in OECD countries. The US is simultaneously the world's largest *recipient* of FDI (with inflows in 1995 of 60 billion dollars) and the largest *source* of FDI (with outflows in excess of 95 billion dollars).

◆　Figure I.　***Private investment flows to developing countries***
(US$ millions)

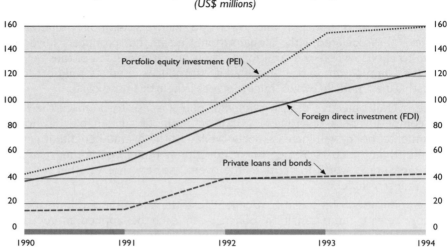

Source: Yale Center for Environmental Law and Policy; World Debt Tables (1996).

While North-to-North capital flows far exceed North-to-South flows, the developing world receives a significant (and growing) share of global FDI. In 1995, developing countries took in approximately 38% of world-wide FDI. However, only a small number of countries are receiving most of the FDI which is going to developing countries. Several recently-industrialised countries are also among the world's largest recipients (*e.g.* Mexico, Singapore, South Korea, Turkey).

The uneven distribution of FDI flows is even further emphasised when geographic location is considered. Between 1989 and 1994, 60% of FDI going to non-OECD countries went to Asia, and 27% to Latin America. A mere 6% went to the whole of Africa. Within regions, the uneven distribution is again apparent. More than half of all FDI inflows to Asia end up in China. In Latin America, a somewhat wider range of countries is being serviced. Mexico and Argentina have been the largest recipients of foreign capital in recent years, although Argentina's inflows were sharply down in 1994, reflecting a general slowdown in the pace of privatisation in that country.

Aggregate data on which economic sectors and/or industries are receiving FDI is not generally available, but some information is available for certain countries. Thus, much of Mexico's FDI has gone recently to the automobile sector; much of China's into industry and real estate. Many countries have tried to attract foreign direct investment by establishing special "free trade zones" for manufacturing.

There is very little data available on how successful these initiatives have been, although it has been reported that one-seventh of all foreign investment dollars in China go into the special economic zones (SEZs) that have been created to promote export industries. Investment in the Costa Rican manufacturing free zones also increased sharply between 1986 and 1995.

One important FDI dynamic relates to competition for limited foreign funds among jurisdictions. In some countries, local leaders have been known to offer potential foreign investors preferential treatment for locating in their jurisdictions.[26] This can include a tacit (or express) commitment to relax the enforcement of environmental standards.

How competitiveness pressures actually play out in the realm of foreign investment also varies from industry to industry. In more "commodity"-like industries, where products are relatively undifferentiated, small cost differences can translate into large changes in market share. Investment flows in these industries may therefore be quite susceptible to differences in the level of environmental standards.

Where investors are competing to get into an expanding market (e.g. China), local entrepreneurs may bargain from a position of strength. For example, in the competition to fund electricity generation projects in some developing countries, western companies have found themselves under pressure to eliminate environmental components from their proposed bids, in order to cut costs.[27] Investors are sometimes told quite clearly that, if *they* are unwilling to proceed on the basis of low environmental costs, *others* are not. In other circumstances, it is the foreign investors themselves who seek to have their environmental requirements relaxed, in order to reduce costs.

Competitiveness pressures can also work in the opposite direction, causing overseas investors to push for *higher* environmental standards. For example, foreign investors in Costa Rican banana production have insisted upon "due environmental care", perceiving that their European customers want an environmentally-sound product.[28]

On the one hand, foreign investors sometimes bring with them modern *technologies* that are improvements (in environmental terms) over what is currently available in the country in which they are investing. Indeed, multinational enterprises frequently build state-of-the-art facilities with the latest (low-polluting) technologies. They also employ advanced environmental management systems and conduct pollution prevention and control training programs. Thus, FDI-based economic expansion offers the promise of significant longer-term environmental improvements.

There are a few isolated examples where it appears that companies have actually dismantled outdated facilities in an industrialised country, and moved them to a developing country. For example, the town and village enterprises (TVEs) of rural China have sometimes purchased used (*i.e.* high-polluting) equipment from industrialised countries.[29] However, most examples of this type of arrangement appear to have originated in other developing countries, rather than in the OECD. Moreover, most cases of "technology dumping" do not implicate FDI at all, but involve simple *sales* of outdated equipment from overseas companies to companies in developing countries.[30]

Environment and FDI: the macroeconomic perspective

Another major political concern is whether higher environmental standards in some countries encourage industry to move to jurisdictions with less expensive environmental regimes ("pollution haven" hypothesis). The main fear is that some countries may be using low environmental standards to attract investment. Two methods have been used to examine this question. The first looks at overseas investment statistics to see if patterns can be found linking offshore investments with environmental standards. The second looks at investment location decision-making processes within the firm, to determine the relative importance of environmental factors in those decisions.[31]

Most overseas investments from industrialised countries in pollution-intensive industries are being made in other developed countries, not in the developing ones. For example, Canada was the largest recipient of total US direct investment abroad in the chemical and mineral processing industries over the period 1982-91.[32] Even in the developing countries, the amount of inward investment in the pollution-intensive industries was a smaller proportion of the total in 1992 than it was two decades earlier, despite the fact that environmental standards in those countries had increased significantly in the interim.[33]

The increased pollution-intensity being observed in developing countries is *consistent with* a "pollution haven" hypothesis, but it does not demonstrate *causality*. As discussed earlier (Sections 1 and 3), the shift into manufacturing industries may be a "normal" part of the development process, and may have little to do with the relative stringency of environmental policies.

Analyses of *decision-making processes* at the level of the firm point to the many factors involved in investment location decisions (*e.g.* political stability, size and growth potential of market, access to other markets, labour costs, ease of repatriation of profits). Most available research suggests that environmental standards play no significant part in investment location decisions. One study of 173 Japanese companies[34] concluded that, although companies complain about high production costs at home, this seldom drives them to actually invest overseas. Meeting overseas demands, or following competitors to new markets, were found to be much more decisive factors.

In this regard, one 1992 study estimated that 85% of US industries have environmental compliance costs that amount to less than 2% of their value-added.[35] Even in industries with high pollution control costs, companies often face significant deterrents to relocation, including high fixed capital investments, and the need to remain close to their markets.

Although not all research arrives at precisely the same conclusion,[36] it therefore appears that there is no discernible pattern of *systematic* investment in LDC "pollution havens". On the other hand, there is evidence that *some* "resource-seeking" firms (see box), especially those facing higher-than-average pollution control costs, *do* move abroad to take advantage of lower costs (which may or may not be due to lower environmental standards) in the host country.

In addition, the threat of industrial relocations is often used by all types of firms who would like to receive reductions in the impact of environmental policies affecting their operations. This threat is sometimes enough to convince policy-makers not to impose new environmental regulations, or to reduce the ones which already exist. In effect, the *threat* of industrial migration (rather than its *reality)* may be generating a "political drag" on improved environmental policy-making in OECD countries.

A different question concerns the relationship between the *degree of openness* in trade and foreign investment regimes and pollution-intensive development. In principle, if trade encourages "pollution havens", the more open developing economies should have relatively higher levels of pollution-intensive development. However, evidence from Latin America indicates that, over the 1970s and 1980s, the more open economies actually ended up with a *cleaner* set of industries. While pollution-intensity grew more rapidly in Latin America as a whole after environmen-

---

Three types of FDI

- **"Market-seeking" FDI.** Many foreign investors are seeking opportunities to sell in overseas markets. The rapid expansion of foreign investment in China can be partly explained by the attraction of that nation's very large (and rapidly-growing) domestic demand.

- **"Resource-seeking" FDI.** Some investors' overseas activities are aimed at access to critical resources that are not available in their own markets. Indeed, the prospect of obtaining access to cheap raw materials is the classic reason for foreign investment (although most FDI today is attracted more by low *wage* costs).

- **"Platform-seeking" FDI.** In some cases, investors set up overseas facilities to serve specific export markets (*i.e.* to provide a "platform" for production and sales activities in a regional market. Recent investments by Japanese auto-makers in the United Kingdom and Mexico, providing "platforms" for sales in the European and North American markets, are obvious examples.

tal regulation in OECD countries became stricter, openness to foreign technology and capital generally seems to facilitate improved environmental performance. The provocative conclusion is therefore reached that, if "pollution havens" *do* exist, they may exist mostly in *protectionist* economies.

Research also suggests[37] that those developing countries which operate straightforward, transparent, and efficient environmental programs experience no loss of FDI, and may even *attract* some industries that want reliable overseas bases of operation. For example, even though Mexico has significantly increased its environmental enforcement efforts over the past few years, FDI in the Mexico City area has expanded rapidly – and air quality has *improved*. Reflecting a similar spirit, a recent survey[38] of multinational investors in Mexico found that most companies felt that reduced subsidies for power and water, along with more consistent enforcement of existing pollution control requirements were the most effective steps the Mexican Government could take to improve industry's environmental performance.

There is little evidence of countries systematically setting higher environmental standards for projects funded by foreign investors. FDI-backed companies typically face the same environmental requirements that any company doing business in that country would be required to meet. Nor is there evidence of the country-of-origin of the foreign investor imposing *direct* environmental requirements on its corporations doing business abroad.

Several countries *do*, however, impose *indirect* environmental restrictions on companies doing business abroad, at least to the extent that these companies benefit from national export finance programmes or aid funds (some of which contain environmental provisions in their project approval criteria).[39]

Similarly, environmental performance requirements are an increasingly important element in the approval criteria used by international institutions. The International Finance Corporation (IFC), the World Bank, the EBRD, and other multilateral development banks (MDB) now routinely incorporate environmental conditions into their screening processes for new investments.[40] Although these standards apply officially only to the funds being provided by the multilateral agency, the MDB standards often become a *de facto* requirement for all participants in a project.

Environment and FDI: the microeconomic perspective

Although it is difficult to isolate the FDI-driven aspects of environmental performance from other causes, it seems that foreign investors meet the environmental standards of the foreign countries in which they operate more often than domestic companies do.[41] This probably reflects the fact that foreign investors expect to be subjected to a greater degree of scrutiny than local companies with regard to their environmental performance.

Very few companies invest overseas with reduced environmental compliance costs as their primary goal.[42] While establishing a low-cost base of operations may be an important reason for setting up operations abroad, in general, multinational enterprises generally seek *consistent*, rather than *lax*, environmental enforcement.

Available data also suggests[43] that *privatisation* (a major source of FDI in many countries) can yield significant environmental *benefits* in some circumstances. Privatised companies are often better managed than public ones, which can result in reduced waste and lower pollution. On the other hand, privatisation can also reduce government control over the environmental behaviour of firms. In some jurisdictions (and some industries), this might lead to *negative* environmental consequences.

One matter of particular importance is the potential FDI recipient's *environmental liability* rules. If excessive burdens are placed on new enterprises for the clean-up of past contamination, foreign investment may be deterred. In Central and Eastern Europe in particular, liability rules appear to have played a major role in determining where FDI was directed, as investors avoided countries that tried to make new owners responsible for cleaning up past toxic contamination.[44]

5.   TRADE[45]

The globalisation process focuses attention on three main issues in the trade-environment linkage:

- What are the probable *environmental* impacts of trade liberalisation and/or protectionism?

- What are the probable *trade* effects of the more stringent environmental measures that might be needed to protect against these impacts?

- How might trade and environment policy integration at the international level contribute to the environmentally-sustainable globalisation of the economy?

The volume of world merchandise trade increased at an average annual rate of slightly more than 6% during the period 1950-94, compared with close to 4% for world output.[46] Although a slower rate of increase in the "trade intensity" of the global economy was experienced between 1974-84, it has once again been intensifying since then. In 1990-95, the annual percentage change in world merchandise exports was four times the growth rate of world merchandise production.

Most of this increase has occurred in the manufacturing sector, especially in *intra-industry* trade. For example, the share of intra-industry trade in total manufacturing trade exceeded 50% in most West European countries in 1991, and has been increasing since then. Intra-*industry* trade is somewhat related to intra-*firm* trade. The latter is now estimated to represent about one-third of world trade. Exports of multinational firms to non-affiliates account for another third, with the remaining third involving trade among national firms.

Environmental impacts of trade liberalisation[47]

"In general terms, trade liberalisation will have a positive effect on the environment by improving the efficient allocation of resources, promoting economic growth and increasing general welfare, provided that effective environmental policies are implemented. OECD governments view trade liberalisation as a positive agent which could provide resources for environmental improvement, particularly for developing countries and countries in transition.

In the absence of effective environmental policies, including those aiming at internalising environmental costs, or when distortionary domestic policies exist, increased economic activity generated from trade liberalisation can contribute to environmental problems. The environmental effects of trade liberalisation – both positive and negative – will vary, depending on the country, sector and particular circumstances."[48]

By increasing the *scale* of economic activity, trade liberalisation can induce *positive* environmental effects (via increased growth and incomes). However, where appropriate policies to protect the environment are *not* in place (or again, where distortionary economic policies exist), the increased scale of economic activity can also result in environmental *degradation* (e.g. from the unsustainable exploitation of natural resources or from increased transportation). The *net* scale effect will therefore depend on the amount of environmental damage induced by the original expansion in economic activity, relative to the positive effects related to the increased demand for environmental quality which could follow increases in incomes.

As discussed earlier (Section 1), there is some empirical evidence suggesting that the amount of environmental regulation and/or environmental quality increases with growth in incomes. On the other hand, there is research indicating that this correlation varies significantly across different measures of environmental *quality*, with those effects which are most *localised* (*i.e.* local air and water pollution) tending to exhibit the most evident inverted-U relationships, and those effects which are more *diffuse* (e.g. greenhouse gases) not exhibiting any such a relationship at all.

Thus, the positive effects of income levels on environmental quality may be weaker, the more "public" the environmental good involved. It also appears that the "turning-point" for some developing countries is much higher than current income levels, so the environment-intensity of production may have to continue to rise for some time in these countries. Moreover, even if the inverted-U relationship *does* hold for particular pollutants, and for a broad group of countries over a particular period of time, it may not be true indefinitely, nor for the world as a whole. Given the possibility that environmental irreversibilities may already be occurring, this is not a very optimistic prospect.

Structural shifts will also be generated by trade liberalisation. One globalisation-related structural shift has already occurred, with the greatly-increased participation of the newly industrialised economies in the international economy. The recent trade-oriented growth in these countries has resulted from a general shift away from primary commodity production, and toward resource-processing, light manufacturing and service activities.

The environmental consequences of these shifts may be considerable. For example, there is some evidence that, once a country begins to industrialise, trade liberalisation tends to make the structure of the economy less pollution-intensive than in those countries whose economies remain relatively closed.[49] In particular, the transition from heavy resource-processing sectors to light manufacturing ones (at middle-income levels) seems to play an important role in reducing the pollution-intensity of the economy. On the other hand, if pollution-intensive production simply shifts to some other country, the environmental impact may simply be *shifted*, rather than being *reduced*.

Trade in environmentally-preferred products, particularly eco-efficient capital equipment and its accompanying "clean" production technologies, is another important mechanism through which globalisation may ultimately benefit the environment. Trade liberalisation may help expand the potential market for environmentally-preferred final products, such as low-emission vehicles, organic foods, and recyclable materials. It should also improve access to environmentally-preferable raw material inputs, such as low- (as opposed to high-) sulphur coal.

Trade liberalisation can also effect the environment via its influence on environmental standards and policies. For example, trade liberalisation agreements may help to promote convergence in national environmental standards (see Section 2). Regional trade liberalisation agreements may also be catalysts for improving the level and enforcement of environmental regulations. In this regard, NAFTA has demonstrated how a complementary package of increased market access and enhanced environmental policy can be constructed.

Trade effects of environmental measures

The economic integration associated with globalisation implies that policy areas traditionally regarded as being "domestic" will increasingly have international ramifications. Environmental policy is one of these areas. For example, a tax levied on large cars, with the aim of reducing energy consumption, will also favour small-car producers at the same time. If the domestic industry produces small cars, while bigger ones are imported, suspicions of trade protectionism may arise.

The most common area of overlap between environmental measures and trade interests is that of national requirements that *products* meet certain environmental, safety, and health standards. Under current multilateral trade rules, these requirements are acceptable, subject to agreed rules. Similarly, taxes and charges applied to *domestic* products can also be applied to similar *imported* products (or exempted on *exports*).

The trade issues become more complex when the various stages of the product's life cycle are at issue (*i.e. processes and production methods* – PPMs). For example, recent packaging and recycling requirements which address environmental issues, but which are associated with the disposal stage of the product life cycle, have caused some trade concerns. This is because waste reduction policies tend to have a national focus, and can thereby impose relatively higher costs on importers, amounting to *de facto* protection for domestic producers.

Emission controls, catch limitations, and specified production techniques are other examples of PPM-related requirements which attempt to mitigate environmental impacts. Trade issues arise if a country attempts to transfer these environmental requirements to imported products in the form of either product-based standards, or equivalent taxes or charges. Particular problems have arisen where countries have sought to enforce particular production methods on activities outside their territorial jurisdictions.

A distinction is made here between *product-related* and *non-product-related* PPMs, as well as between environmental impacts occurring at the national, transboundary or global level. Product-related PPMs are those which affect the *characteristics of the product*. Non-product related PPMs do not affect product characteristics, but generate an environmental impact at the *production stage* (*e.g.* emissions).

To date, trade rules have been interpreted as precluding policy differentiation on the basis of non-product-related PPM requirements. Similarly, adjusting the price of imported products at the border, to account for the additional costs incurred by domestic industry in complying with non-product-related PPM requirements, has generally been considered to be incompatible with existing trade rules.

It is important to recognise that the rules (and their interpretations) concerning border tax adjustment (BTA) have been developed primarily in the context of *domestic* environmental issues and measures. The trading system is now also having to deal with *global* environmental problems. Imposing costs on domestic industry for the benefit of a global public good is politically difficult, since it raises competitiveness concerns, and it may not even be environmentally effective if the means of production are mobile ("leakage" problem). Therefore "neutralising" policies are often considered (*e.g.* either exempting energy-intensive/export-oriented industries entirely from the environmental policy, or subsiding their compliance costs). In this context, BTAs may sometimes be a preferable policy option. The use of border tax adjustment in conjunction with domestic (process-related) taxes aimed at reducing global environmental damage (*e.g.* from greenhouse gas emissions) is currently under consideration in some countries for this reason. The OECD has therefore concluded that the practical feasibility, environmental benefits, and potential risk of disguised protectionism associated with adjusting taxes on the basis of production processes and inputs at the border are not yet clear, and require further exploration.

Globalisation, combined with the continued growing importance of environmental issues, will intensify the conflict between the traditional "a product is its physical characteristics" perspective, and a "life-cycle" perspective, which seeks to address environmental externalities wherever they may originate. On the one hand, consumers increasingly want to know about the overall environmental impact of their purchases. For globally-integrated production chains (*e.g.* the automotive industry), some component suppliers are already being asked to supply products made using methods laid down by the purchaser (see Section 8). At the moment, this is being done largely to ensure consistency in product quality, but it could eventually apply to environmental criteria as well.

Thus, there is some pressure in the direction of a "life cycle" perspective. On the other hand, national-level trade policies that discriminate against imported products on the basis of their production methods also raise fundamental issues of national sovereignty – issues which are extremely difficult to reconcile with the more globally-oriented "life-cycle" view.

Integration of international environmental and trade agreements

Efforts to apply various international policies to sustainable development objectives have intensified in recent years. This is at least partially attributable to the more globalised nature of economic activity. *Trade policy* is one of the areas where better integration has been proposed. On the *multilateral* trade front, for example, both the OECD and the WTO CTE have recently affirmed[50] the possibility that trade measures *could* be used in certain cases to achieve environmental objectives, especially when trade is directly related to the source of the environmental problem.

Regional trade agreements are also paying more attention to the possibility of integrating environmental and trade policies, with the NAFTA side-agreement on the environment being a prominent recent example. (ASEAN, the European Union, and APEC provide other examples). In the case of NAFTA, Mexico, Canada and the US undertook the unprecedented action of analysing the potential environmental consequences of the accord prior to its adoption. The NAFTA side-agreement on the environment also created a Commission for Environmental Co-operation, which is authorised to monitor environmental programmes in NAFTA countries.

6. SECTORAL ECONOMIC ACTIVITIES[51]

The energy, agriculture and transport sectors not only account for a high percentage of global economic output. They also account for a large percentage of the environmental impacts that may result from a more global approach to producing and consuming that output. Trade liberalisation, privatisation, deregulation, and other globalisation-induced policy reforms are likely to affect each of these three sectors in different ways.

In thinking about the environment and globalisation-induced changes in sectoral economic activities, it is worth recalling the distinction made earlier (Section 1) between economic *development* and economic *globalisation*. This distinction has particular relevance in the context of sectoral activities. For example, increasing world energy consumption – particularly the consumption of fossil fuels – is only partially attributable to globalisation. Most of this increase derives from the economic development process more generally.

Not all of the important relationships between globalisation and the environment in the energy, transport, and agriculture sectors are covered by a focus on liberalisation policies. However, the following examples based on recent movements toward trade liberalisation and deregulation at least illustrate the nature of the globalisation-environment linkage in each sector.

Deregulation and privatisation in electricity generation[52]

Competition associated with globalisation is intensifying the search for ways of reducing energy costs, especially the costs of electricity. Many countries have therefore eased entry restrictions on electricity generation activities since the 1980s, and taken steps to increase competition in electricity pricing regimes.

Deregulation and privatisation of electricity production will intensify the pressure for using cheapest fuel, which may be cleaner or dirtier, depending on national circumstances. These *fuel-switching* effects can sometimes be very significant for the environment. In the UK, for example, significant limits once existed on the use of gas in electricity generation. After deregulation, the share of natural gas in power generation rose from 1% in 1990, to 11% in 1993 (expected to rise to 46 % by 2010). This shift is proving to be a major factor in the ability of the UK to meet its greenhouse gas emission reduction objectives.

Under other circumstances, however, deregulation (and lower prices) could encourage shifts in the direction of "dirtier" fuels. For example, electricity deregulation in both the US and Japan are expected to generate *increased* use of (relatively cheaper) coal and oil resources – a shift which would likely produce *negative* environmental consequences.

Increased competition in electricity also encourages suppliers to seek improvements in energy efficiency, which may reduce both emissions and the new investments in additional capacity that would have otherwise been required. On the other hand, there may also be pressure to ease existing conservation-oriented regulations for electricity suppliers.[53] For example, many States in the US have established programmes to encourage consumers to conserve energy or to use more efficient energy sources. After deregulation, States may be more reluctant to require utilities to continue to pay for such programmes.

Deregulation is also expected to reduce the price of electricity, which may lower the use of (relatively more expensive) renewable energy sources, such as solar and wind power. These structural changes in turn, may induce extra resource depletion and/or increased greenhouse gas emissions. They may also mean that new hydropower and nuclear projects become less economic, again implying some shift to more emission-intensive technologies.

Lower prices will also probably lead to an increase in electricity consumption overall, producing a negative scale effect. A key question will be whether this negative effect is larger than any emission reductions which may be achieved through fuel-switching and/or increased energy efficiencies. The specific characteristics of a country's energy market, coupled with its environmental policy regime, will determine the net result.

Trade in electricity[54]

Electricity is increasingly a traded commodity. This is due to reduced restrictions on trans-border flows. Most of Europe is now linked in its electricity grid as far east as Poland, with connections reaching across the Balkans to Turkey. An extension is also planned to North Africa (via the Mediterranean Ring). Despite the high costs of transmitting electricity over long distances, the large differentials which exist between electricity prices in different regions create significant potential for trade.

Some positive environmental impacts might result from this increased trade in electricity. For example, in the "transition" economies of Central and Eastern Europe (EITs), greater trade in electricity may contribute to increased pressure on the EITs from Western European energy producers (and their consumers) to raise their environmental standards. Both fuel-switching and efficiency-based environmental improvements could be part of these shifts.

On the other hand, there are also concerns that increased electricity trade with EIT countries might undercut industrial electricity prices in Western Europe, thereby displacing "cleaner" suppliers located there. The potential scale of this problem is revealed by the example of Poland, where heavily-polluting "hard" coal and lignite accounted for 96 % of 1992 electricity generation. However, two factors may help to limit this effect. First, the effect may be transitory, as short-term prospects for EITs to exploit differences in environmental standards give way to longer-term obligations to increase environmental standards. Second, existing regulatory barriers within the EU are planned to remain in place until 1998.

Emergence of Independent Power Producers[55]

Another important globalisation-related development in the energy sector has been the emergence of a competitive international market for electricity produced by Independent Power Producers (IPPs). This phenomenon originated from important regulatory changes in the US, which allowed IPPs to sell their electricity to utilities. The idea of using IPPs to help increase competition in electricity supply soon spread, and IPPs are now building power plants in developing countries. Because state-owned utilities in developing countries often lack the funds to build new plants, and because demand for power in many developing countries is rapidly increasing, the IPPs are enjoying an expanding market. Between 1991 and 1994, over 25 "green-field" deals for US-based IPPs to build power plants (50 megawatts or larger) were closed in the Asia/Pacific and Latin American Regions.[56]

In principle, IPPs might provide environmental benefits by installing cleaner production technologies in developing country power plants. However, more than half of the IPP projects completed as of 1994 in developing countries involved coal plants. If a developing country has coal, no natural gas, and not very stringent SO_2 emission standards, it is unlikely that an IPP will be in a position to incur the additional costs of installing expensive coal scrubbers, let alone gas turbines. A new plant built by an IPP in a developing country is therefore likely to contain virtually the same technology as one built by a domestic utility.

Moreover, the development of an international market for independent power has already resulted in the construction of more power plants in developing countries, and therefore more pollution, than would otherwise have occurred (scale effect). And, as noted above, the IPP market may still be growing, implying that this negative environmental impact may continue for some time, assuming that no additional environmental action is taken by host countries.

This last point emphasises the important role that technology transfer activities by developed countries might play in conjunction with IPP activities. In effect, IPPs could become important vectors for technical advice on electricity generation technologies, on the *operation* of these technologies, or on *management methods* provided that this advice were made available to all competitors in these developing country markets.

Energy-intensive industries[57]

Between 1973 and 1993, industrial energy demand in OECD countries declined 0.4 % per year, while it has increased by 5% each year in East and South Asia. In addition, energy-intensive industries (such as steel) declined in OECD countries, while previous steel importers (*e.g.* Brazil, Korea) became important exporters.

There is considerable debate about the reason for these shifts. On the one hand, energy-intensity in developing countries would be expected to increase "naturally", as the economy shifts out of agriculture and into industrial production. Similarly, developed economies would be expected to shift away from industry and toward services. These factors may explain why energy-intensive industries seem to be "migrating" to developing countries.

On the other hand, it is also possible that this shift is at least partially due to differences in energy costs (part of which can be attributed to *environmental* considerations, via excise and other taxes, for example). In the specific case of iron and steel, the cost of energy *does* appear to have played some role in the shift away from OECD countries. "Resource-seeking" industries (Section 4) in particular (*e.g.* non-ferrous metal smelting and refining operations) have revealed this tendency. The price of electricity is particularly important in the aluminium smelting industry, accounting for almost 30% of operating costs.

Because industrial energy demand accounts for more than one-third of world final energy consumption, trends in energy use among large industrial users (*e.g.* iron and steel) may also have important environmental ramifications. For example, if less energy-efficient steel-making technologies are employed when steel producers move to non-OECD countries, more energy will be consumed and more pollution will be emitted. There is also the possibility that steel-makers operating in non-OECD countries may be subject to less stringent regulatory controls.

On the other hand, the fact that new investments are being made also provides an opportunity for more environmentally-friendly technologies to be used in the new plants. There is some evidence[58] that the aluminium industry, in particular, has taken advantage of these "technological renovation" opportunities when relocating their facilities.

Deregulation of freight transport[59]

Trade liberalisation in general, and freight transport *deregulation* in particular, are both likely to lead to lower freight costs across most transport modes in most countries. Even where transport costs rise in the short term (*e.g.* Central and Eastern Europe), the longer-term pressure on costs is likely to be downwards. Reduced costs, combined with the increased incomes that should result from a more efficient transport system generally, are likely to result in new demands for transport services. In turn, new demands for transport services may lead to new environmental stresses in the form of noise, air pollution, and congestion (*scale effects*), once again under the assumption that no additional action is taken to protect the environment.

While road freight has been expanding rapidly in recent years, rail and inland shipping freight traffic have remained relatively static. The net result has been a significant increase in market share going to the road mode. This trend is not very encouraging from an environmental perspective, since the rail and waterway modes are often regarded as being more environmentally-benign than road transport. This shift has been aided by the significant deregulation that has occurred in the road sector since 1980.

In the US, for example, the cost of intercity freight transport fell dramatically (from 7.8 to 6.3% of GDP) after the significant deregulations which occurred there during the 1980s. At the same time, the average length of freight hauls was increasing. Much of this saving resulted from freight now being carried by more efficient modes, but some derived from technological changes, such as the expanded use of unit trains.

Deregulation in the US *rail* sector has also led directly to lower costs (an average decline of 1.5% per annum after 1980) and to service improvements. As a result, rail freight's energy use declined by 26 % between 1980 and 1993, even while ton-miles were increasing by 27%. Part of this improvement was due to the improved financial status of railroads, which now had the capacity to purchase more energy-efficient locomotives. Deregulation also resulted in the abandonment of many kilometres of track, often in favour of more environmentally-friendly land uses.

Trucking deregulation is also estimated to have saved the (US) industry about 23% of 1980 costs by 1984. One result of the rationalisation which occurred was that fewer heavy-duty trucks came to be used, involving fewer back-hauls, and thus, more efficient use of energy.

Air cargo has grown the most rapidly of all modes since deregulation. The air sector has also witnessed significant structural changes, since much package traffic which used to go by air now goes by road, given the increases in service quality that have occurred within the latter mode.

Another result of deregulation in the US has been that *intermodal* freight transport options are also now being more actively exploited. In particular, rail-barge movements have expanded considerably. Combined with restructuring in the rail industry, expansion and deregulation in the road haulage and aviation industries, these changes made a significant contribution to the carrying values of US inventories, with concomitant savings in operating costs.

A recent OECD study[60] suggests that the environmental effects of freight transport deregulation in the US may have been *positive* (at least in terms of the freight *movements* themselves). Less total energy is now used by railroads than in 1980. Double-stack trains have increased the competitiveness of rail, thereby slowing the shift toward the less environmentally-sensitive road mode. The shift toward intermodal transfer has also helped to reduce road congestion. Even the road hauliers now use much less energy per ton-mile now than they did in 1980. This is because more back-hauls are now possible, because of technological advances in the trucks themselves, and because of infrastructure improvements.

On the other hand, even though freight deregulation may be producing *some* positive structural and technological effects for the environment in terms of freight *movements*, there may be other negative structural effects being generated in terms of the *products* being transported. For example, lower US rail freight prices may result in coal becoming more competitive in energy markets, across longer distances with potentially *negative* environmental impacts.

The way in which transport deregulation has proceeded in Europe has been quite different from the approach taken in the US.[61] Road and rail deregulation occurred almost simultaneously in the US, whereas European deregulation has so far concentrated mainly on road transport. The net result is that road transport has been able to profit more than proportionally from the growing European transport market. Inland waterways and pipelines have retained their (small) market shares, while the rail mode has been the major loser.

The modal shift in favour of the road has been achieved at the expense of additional environmental stresses at the local, regional, and global levels. One approach to reducing this stress might be to speed up the process of rail deregulation, perhaps in combination with more privatisation of the industry. Europe is clearly moving in this direction, but change is occurring slowly. This is at least partially due to the fact that market conditions and rail sector infrastructures in Europe are fundamentally different from those in North America. Rail deregulation in Europe would therefore not be a matter of simply transposing principles that may have worked well in North America.

There are also continuing problems related to the *enforcement* of environmental regulations in the freight sector. Such is the ferocity of competition in the European road haulage industry, for example, that serious concerns are often raised about the ability of governments to enforce those environmental regulations which *do* exist.

The shift toward *road* freight in Europe has led to increased environmental tensions in some countries. "Transit" countries (*e.g.* Austria, Belgium, Hungary, and Switzerland) in particular are likely to suffer additional noise, air pollution and infrastructure costs associated with globalisation-induced road haulage, without generating proportionate economic benefits to cover these additional costs. In partial response, Austria has introduced an "eco-point" quota system, as well as special motorway tolls for travel across environmentally-sensitive roads (e.g. Brenner Pass). Switzerland maintains a strict weight regulation for trucks, and has recently passed legislation which will require truck traffic to use combined transport facilities in the future (road-rail).

Effects of trade liberalisation on freight transport

It is generally anticipated that reduced trade barriers will lead to increased international freight transport (i.e. scale effects). A recent OECD study[62] examined the size of this effect, and concluded that even full implementation of all import tariff reduction commitments contained in the Uruguay Round would only lead to an increase in the global volume of traded goods of only some 3-4%, with the volume of international freight transport increasing only slightly more (at 4-5%).

Some sectors would experience large increases in *trade* volumes, but not necessarily in *transport* requirements. In the agriculture sector, for example, the new output generated by trade liberalisation would be transported shorter distances than current (subsidised) production. On the other hand, the large increase in textile outputs would be associated with more than proportional increases in international transport. The modelling results also indicate that US exports and Asian imports would show the largest transport-related growth. European agriculture-related transport would decline, but Japanese agriculture-related transport would increase. Textile-related transport would increase in all regions.

The main message to be derived from these results is that the scale effect of trade liberalisation may be relatively small, when compared with the additional transport which may be required to service normal economic growth. Macro-economic projections of total increases in transport to the year 2004 (the year that full implementation of the Uruguay Round commitments is anticipated) suggest a 71% increase over 1992 levels. This is approximately *15 times* the growth expected to result from trade liberalisation, based on the result of the above simulation. This conclusion is reinforced by the fact that international trade movements remain small, compared to overall movements of freight (i.e. including domestic freight).

However, it should *not* be inferred from these results that the scale effects of trade liberalisation will not harm the environment. In principle, *any* increase in freight traffic will bring *absolute* increases in environmental damages with it (scale effects). The *rate* of increase may be lowered, but environmental harms will still grow absolutely. For another thing, the scale effects will probably be larger in some countries than they are in others. In particular, transit countries are already finding that trade liberalisation is increasing the volume of traffic on their networks. Thus, scale effects will have different environmental impacts in different countries, and those countries with the highest impacts may find that the costs of these impacts are significant.

Negative *product effects* might also be anticipated from trade liberalisation in the freight sector. As in the case of deregulation, trade liberalisation should lower freight prices, making it cheaper to transport some goods (especially bulk goods) that had previously been impeded by higher prices. The obvious example is coal (see above), which may gain a larger market because of price reductions. More coal consumption implies more greenhouse gas and acid rain emissions.

On the other hand, it is conceivable that *positive* (*i.e.* environmentally-friendly) technological and/or structural changes in the freight sector could result from trade liberalisation. For example, NAFTA is helping to reorient North American transport toward a more rational economic pattern (*e.g.* from an east-west axis, toward a north-south one). More open borders should allow shippers to use the most efficient routes to reach their markets. This should further increase the attractiveness of low-energy water routes, such as the *Intercoastal Waterway* and the Mississippi River for shipping goods which originate in Mexico or Canada.

NAFTA is also opening up new opportunities to make transportation decisions based on the real economic value of the land resources, rather than on the distorted signals generated by subsidised markets. For example, the elimination of the Crow Rate freight subsidy in Canada is likely to reduce agricultural pressure on marginal lands. This may also lead to reductions in agricultural intensities on those lands (*e.g.* reduced reliance on pesticides and herbicides). All of these changes imply positive *structural effects* for the environment.

On the technology side, one study has suggested that already-available engine technologies could eventually result in fuel-economy improvements of about 10-20% betwen 1985 and 2000. However, this does not necessarily translate into environmental improvements. For example, average US fuel efficiencies for heavy duty vehicles *did* increase by about 10 per cent between 1982 and 1987, but then levelled off between 1987 and 1992. Increased truck sizes (after deregulation), higher speed limits, and reduced diesel fuel prices probably each contributed to this reduced rate of improvement. In effect, new engine technologies *are* available, but... "more R&D will be necessary before (they) can be reliably and cost-effectively incorporated into the fleet".[63]

Regulatory reform of transport in Central and Eastern Europe[64]

Freight volumes in Central and Eastern Europe dropped sharply (about one-third) after the reforms which took place in 1989, but have rebounded in recent years. Economic recovery and closer ties with the EU are both expected to lead to considerable freight traffic growth in future years.

Despite a general increase in car ownership, total passenger traffic has als[o] fallen (although less rapidly than the rate of decline in freight volumes). It is i[n] passenger volumes that the effects of rising petrol and other operating prices an[d] reduced incomes are the most visible. In the rail sector, fares have also increase[d] significantly, thereby limiting passenger demand. However, rail fares are still con[n]siderably lower than those in Western Europe.

In terms of modal split, the share of rail freight virtually collapsed in mos[t] countries after reform, with road being the primary beneficiary of this shift. Rail los[t] between one- and two-thirds of its freight volume between 1989 and 1994, depend[d]ing on the country involved.

Economic integration is also revealing significant deficiencies in the transpo[rt] infrastructure of most Central and Eastern European countries. In the road freigh[t] sector for example, there is a very low density of autoroutes, the arteries throug[h] which most road transport occurs in Western Europe. There are also specia[l] problems at international frontiers, where waits of several hours are common. Bot[h] of these trends are creating pressures for new infrastructure, and all of the enviror[n]mental problems that would be associated with it.

One result of the shift toward private automobile use is that *public transpo[rt]* use is declining. For example, public transport in Budapest experienced a decline i[n] market share from 80% to 60% between 1989 and 1994. This is causing specia[l] problems for cities. Urban road networks and parking infrastructures are provin[g] inadequate to service the increased traffic volumes that are being observed. Traffi[c] control systems are also out-of-date. The result is more congestion and highe[r] levels of air pollution and noise.

Economic restructuring is also occurring in the transport sector. The roa[d] haulage industry in particular has experienced rapid privatisation in recent year[s]. One result is the significant "atomisation" of the industry. For example, Poland no[w] has more than 80 000 road haulage enterprises. This has made the *enforcement [of]* environmental regulations in these countries more difficult.

Effects of agricultural trade liberalisation

The *reform of agricultural support programmes* and *agricultural trade libera*[l]*isation* have both been embodied in what may be the single most significant polic[y] change to date in the direction of globalisation – the completion of the 199[4] Uruguay Round negotiations. Pressure for agricultural reform had been mountin[g] throughout the 1980s, with the rapid expansion of both agricultural subsidies an[d] agricultural non-tariff barriers, particularly in the OECD countries. Not only wer[e] these policies proving expensive and inefficient in OECD countries, the developin[g] countries were also suffering from lack of access to important export markets.

Despite the significant step forward represented by the *Agreement on Agriculture*, the task of re-orienting global agriculture toward market forces is far from complete. The tariffs which remain in place even after the Uruguay Round reforms are still high enough to constrain trade. The required reforms also vary from country to country, nor are they comprehensive in their coverage. Many countries continue to rely on production quotas, administered prices, and related border measures (rather than market prices) to guide their production decisions.

The *Agreement on Agriculture* involves significant changes in existing border controls on agricultural products in many WTO countries. For example, penalties will now be imposed on non-tariff import barriers, and constraints will be increased on export subsidies. In addition, all Parties to the *Agreement* must comply with minimum market access commitments.

Agricultural protectionism is often accused of generating overly-intensive domestic production in the OECD countries, which may lead to negative environmental consequences. For example, extra input use and monoculture technologies may both be encouraged.[65] Additional OECD exports may then "crowd" the global market, reducing the returns to agriculture in the developing countries. Key agricultural investments needed in those countries may then be foregone. One result can be the spread of low-yielding farming and ranching techniques into ecologically-vulnerable tropical forests. Trade liberalisation should help to reverse these negative tendencies in most countries (by lowering production intensities, even though these intensities might actually *increase* in those countries where trade restrictions are already relatively low – for example, New Zealand and Argentina).[66]

The scale effects associated with agricultural trade liberalisation could be either positive or negative for the environment. On the one hand, trade liberalisation should increase the scale of agricultural activity more than would be expected from economic growth occurring in the absence of trade liberalisation. To the extent that these new agricultural activities take place in the presence of *inadequate* environmental policies, negative environmental results would follow. On the other hand, the increased overall efficiency that trade liberalisation might generate should reduce the environmental/resource intensity of each unit of output, thereby limiting any scale effects that would otherwise have arisen.

The structural changes that may follow agricultural trade reform could also lead to negative environmental consequences. For example, trade liberalisation might decrease farm-gate prices in some countries, imperilling some of the environmental benefits currently being generated by farmers (*e.g.* countryside management, wildlife habitat, water management benefits). Trade reform might also result in increased demand (via lower prices) for specific agricultural goods that are produced in an "environmentally-unfriendly" way.

Nor would the shift from more *intensive* to more *extensive* agricultural produc tion *necessarily* be entirely positive for the environment. For example, the transfe of production from (more intensive) Europe to (more extensive) developing coun tries might actually increase the rate of land degradation in the latter region, where the environmental "damage potential" for the world as a whole could be particu larly high (*e.g.* biodiversity loss).

On balance, the effects of trade liberalisation on agriculture are *expected* to be generally positive for the environment, *provided* appropriate environmental policie: are in place when the liberalisation occurs.[67] Whether or not these expectations are *actually* realised in practice will depend on several complex factors. Examining thi specific question, a recent OECD report concluded that "the weight of the evidence to date does *not* suggest that production changes under trade liberalisation wil cause broad near-term environmental benefits or damage. *Some* improvements can be expected from agricultural policy reform. But 'pockets of stress' from concen trated production and land abandonment, pest invasions, and problems in non OECD countries, will likely occur. Larger risks lie ten years or more into the future when trade liberalisation is fully implemented and a rapidly-growing world popula tion pushes up food demand and prices. Creating environmental policies for these *uncertain* problems with minimal trade effect presents a major challenge" (empha sis added).[68]

Effects of reforming agricultural support programmes

Over the period 1986/88-95, the structure of agricultural support programme in OECD countries changed considerably. Although the overall level of suppor actually increased, the rate of support tended to fall (or at least to remain stable) The use of *direct payments* for delivering that support also grew, usually at the expense of *output-related* supports. For the OECD as a whole, direct payments as share of total support increased from 18% to 23%, while market price suppor declined from 66% to 58%.[69] The shift away from output supports may be particu larly beneficial for the environment, since incentives to use marginal land fo agricultural purposes should thereby be reduced.

The new international restrictions on subsidised exports should contribute to higher prices for a wide range of key agricultural commodities. Recent polic reforms at the national or regional levels should also contribute to higher worl market prices. The combined effects of reform-induced increases in world prices an decreases in support prices may then reduce differentials between subsidised an unsubsidised markets.

Simulations of even the complete removal of all agricultural support pro grammes world-wide suggest that this would not generate very large impacts o world food output, at least in aggregate. Nor would the relocation of production b very significant. For example, one study[70] reported that grain and meat prices would decrease by an estimated 5-6% in industrialised nations, but would increase 3-8% in the developing countries. Within the OECD group, production would fall considerably in Japan and Europe, but would increase in both North America and Australia. Importantly, in those regions where output would be expected to *decline*, the reductions would be a relatively large proportion of total output; in those regions where *increases* in output were expected, the gains would *not* be a very large proportion of total output.

Some observers see agricultural support policies as the source of a wide range of environmental problems. Examples include:[71]

- *Price or output supports*, usually found in higher-income countries, can raise domestic prices relative to world prices. Higher prices encourage chemical over-use, mechanisation, and land conversion, all of which can harm the environment. In contrast, some low-income countries use pricing mechanisms to protect consumers from high food prices. This effectively taxes farmers and discourages production and investment. Sustainable farming practices may suffer as a result in these countries, and migration to urban centres may be encouraged, placing additional environmental stresses on areas which are already heavily-populated.

- *Input subsidies* reduce the cost of chemicals, irrigation, or credit, and can encourage the over-use of these factors. Over-use can then lead to additional pollution. Similarly, interest subsidies provide incentives to invest more heavily in farm capital, which may also contribute to a shift toward more capital- and stock-intensive farming practices.

- *Land set-aside programmes* restrict the use of a key agricultural input (land), usually to offset the output-increasing effects of price support policies. The result may be that pressure grows to increase the productivity of the land remaining in cultivation. If the higher yields are achieved by using more polluting inputs, production techniques, or cropping patterns, set-asides might work against the environment.

On the other hand, the reform of agricultural support programmes will not *necessarily* lead to environmental improvements. Perhaps the reforms will not be sufficient in themselves; perhaps the agriculture-environment linkages are not as direct as first thought. More specifically:[72]

- Reforms may encourage a switch from low-valued to high-valued crops, with the latter often involving more *intensive* use of pesticides and fertilisers.

- If agricultural policy reforms alter the relative prices of crops that can be grown in rotation, the result may be that crop rotations are discouraged, and that chemical inputs actually *increase* (in order to maintain soil productivity) after reforms have been carried out.

- If any land that is set-aside were to be environmentally-enhanced (perhaps by covering it with perennial vegetation), the positive environmental effects obtained on this land might outweigh any negative effects resulting from the more intensive production on land remaining in cultivation.

- A reduction in support may also lead to the abandonment of previously-productive land. If this also happens to be ecologically-important land that farming activities had previously helped to maintain, the environmental consequences of its abandonment may be negative. Furthermore, the shift in agricultural production may be toward land that has a higher risk of environmental problems (e.g. salinity, soil erosion).

Some countries have also attempted to "target" environmental objectives through the use of "agri-environmental measures". These measures generally take one of two forms: *investments* (aimed directly at environmental goals), and *cross-compliance provisions* (which make eligibility for agricultural support programmes contingent on the fulfilment of certain environmental restrictions).

These programmes *do* contribute to environmental objectives, and they are an increasingly popular element of agricultural support reforms. This is especially true of investment-type measures, which are based on the idea of internalising the external environment *benefits* of farming activities. However, both forms of agri-environmental measure need to be carefully thought out, and seem unlikely to be the most efficient way of protecting the environment over the longer-term.[73] Particular care should be taken not to link these programmes to agricultural *outputs*, because any environmental gains that the programmes would generate might then be "eroded" by the additional (output-related) scale effects.

Another problem with these programmes is that it is difficult to separate the (public) benefits to the environment from the (private) benefits to the farmer. There is therefore a risk that the distortionary effects of support programmes might be prolonged by simply renaming "subsidies" as "environmental payments".

Reducing subsidies to agricultural *outputs* will be an important step in reducing the scale effects of agriculture on the environment. Reducing output subsidies will also have the beneficial effect of reducing the need for some of the agri-environmental measures discussed above. On the other hand, reducing subsidies which have structural effects on land use are less obviously beneficial for the environment.

On balance, the reform of agricultural support programmes is likely to alleviate *some* environmental problems, but *others* will probably persist, and new ones may be created, especially with respect to land use. The net environmental effects will depend on the physical characteristics of this land, as well as on the specific uses to which it is put after the reform process is complete. Reforms will free-up not only land, but other resources as well. The reallocation of these resources to other uses both within and outside the agriculture sector, may or may not benefit the environment *overall*.[74]

7.   TECHNOLOGY CHANGE[75]

Economic globalisation and technological change

In 1994, OECD countries were responsible for 96% of global research and development.[76] It has also been estimated that 80% of foreign direct investment originates in those countries which are the primary sources of new technology (US, UK, Japan, Germany, Netherlands and Switzerland).[77]

It has also been estimated[78] that 75% of international technology transfer arises from *trade flows*. International trade in *capital equipment* is the most direct of these channels, since a large proportion of global trade is in "producer" goods (*i.e.* goods which are used in the production of other goods, and which are therefore important determinants of the production technologies).[79] In 1994, world trade in machinery and transport equipment represented 38% of total global trade – an increase from just over 25% in 1980.[80] This is a faster rate of growth than any other form of manufacture or primary commodity.

By increasing the size of the market, trade and investment liberalisation allow firms to realise technological developments through economies of scale. On the one hand, larger markets mean that there are greater incentives for firms to *innovate*, since they will realise even greater profits from successful innovations than would have been the case in the absence of trade. On the other hand, for those technological developments which require large production runs to be efficient, *diffusion* rates may increase.

Globalisation-induced innovation based on increased competition can also improve the chances that a firm will survive, even where market size is *not* increasing. Competition itself is an incentive for innovation, and innovating firms should be better able to withstand the pressures of an increasingly globalised economy.

MNEs play an important role in these processes. For example, about 75% of global industrial R&D is done by MNEs.[81] Although it has been estimated[82] that only about 10-20% of USMNE R&D is undertaken by affiliates overseas, this amount is growing rapidly. However, this effort is geographically concentrated in other OECD countries – not much of it is yet done in the developing countries.

Neo-classical growth theory hypothesised that technology in the developing countries would eventually "converge" with those used in the developed ones. While there is some empirical support for this view (at least in OECD countries),[83] "new growth theory"[84] (wherein a country's future development trajectory is dependant on its historical path)[85] suggests that technological convergence and diffusion are "driven" mostly by national differences in factor endowments. Since factor endowments (and their costs) differ widely across countries, countries will face very different incentives to generate or adopt particular technologies.

The significance of this is that technologies developed for application in OECD countries may sometimes actually be inefficient when applied to developing country contexts. This may explain some of the observed differences in diffusion rates between OECD countries and LDCs. In extreme cases, it may also lead to "technology enclaves", in which advanced technology is transferred only to particular areas within LDCs.[86]

Another important determinant of a country's technological trajectory relates to its capacity to absorb innovations. In this vein, it has been observed that industrial R&D in host countries by MNEs tends to lag behind foreign direct investment, and that foreign direct investment tends to lag behind industrial development more generally. In effect, it seems that technology is being transferred to countries which already possess the skills and/or endowments necessary to successfully exploit that technology.[87]

Given the importance of similarities in economic conditions and of national capacities to absorb innovations, it is not surprising that it is the OECD countries which have benefited most so far from the technological advances inherent in the globalisation process.[88] Some of the NICs have also benefited from international flows in knowledge and technology, particularly in so-called "mid-tech" sectors,[8] but except for some the simpler technologies (e.g. textiles), the developing countries are not yet fully participating in these benefits.

Technological change and the environment-intensity of production

Since natural capital tends to have been under-priced in the past, it may be that technological progress has been biased toward the use of natural resources. Even if this is so, it may be that the overall rate of technological progress is high enough that the environmental characteristics of *total* technological change are still improving.

At the global level, total world "materials" consumption rose by 38% between 1970 and 1991,[90] while real global GDP rose by 92% in the same period. Figure gives an indication of global trends in the resource-, material- and pollution-intensities of the global economic system, in which several physical indicators of environment-intensity are deflated by real GDP, and then indexed. The results reveal a general decrease in the environment-intensity of production. However, it should be stressed that aggregate figures for *all* indicators consistently rose throughout the same period, suggesting that the negative scale effects may be outweighing any positive technology and/or structural effects.

◆ Figure 2. **Changes in the resource-intensity, material-intensity and pollution-intensity of global economic activity (1980 = 1)**

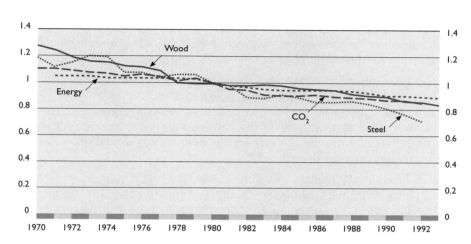

Source: Johnstone (1997).

"Clean" technology innovation can result from changes in products or production processes, from input substitution effects, or from changes in operating procedures.[91] A key determinant of whether or not a particular "clean" innovation will be adopted is its *cost*, but "cost" has many dimensions which need to be considered. For example, investments in "end-of-pipe" equipment may be relatively less costly in *gross* terms, but may represent a larger *net* cost, since process technology improvements often generate secondary environmental and/or economic benefits for the firm.

These *secondary benefits* are increasingly being recognised by industry. Between 1988 and 1994, the proportion of (US) water pollution abatement capital expenditures attributable to changes in the production process, (rather than to "end-of-pipe" abatement) increased from 17% to 30%.[92] The equivalent figures for air pollution capital abatement are even more significant, increasing from 27% to 38%. Thus, it would appear that there has been a significant trend towards more integrated forms of pollution abatement.

Most studies[93] conclude that *regulatory pressure* is the most important demand-side determinant of the environmental intensity of technology. However, a distinction is drawn between *product* and *process* characteristics, with the former not surprisingly being relatively more subject to *customer* pressure.

Only two supply-side factors seem to be very important. First, innovative firms need to be able to appropriate the benefits from any technological developments which mitigate environmental damages. This implies the need for an effective intellectual property rights system.[94] This is particularly important for specialist firms which generate innovations with cross-sectoral applications. Second, the absolute level of industrial R&D may also be an important determinant.

It has been observed[95] that the most active sectors in environment-related industrial R&D are machinery, chemicals, petroleum and motor vehicles. However it was also found that the (1994) proportion of R&D in these sectors in total pollution abatement expenditures in the US was only 1.6%, having declined from 4.9% in 1972. In real terms, therefore, there has been a 1.6% annual *decrease* in R&D related to abatement over this period.[96]

The environmental intensity of technologies can also be influenced through the choice of policy instrument. More specifically, *permits and taxes* are often favoured over *subsidies* (because subsidies are sometimes seen as *compounding* market failures, whereas taxes and permits are seen as *reducing* them). When technological innovation is introduced into the equation, however, the picture is not so clear.

On the one hand, subsidies and taxes/permits may not have equivalent effects. In particular, imperfect capital markets may prevent the adoption of particular innovations. This is thought to be particularly important for SMEs, who may face capital constraints and/or inadequate access to environmental information. There is some empirical evidence[97] at the level of households to suggest that subsidies are more effective than taxes in providing incentives to adopt particular energy conservation measures, so the same reasoning may apply at the level of the firm.

On the other hand, the process of technological innovation may be affected differently by the two measures. This is due to the dual nature of externalities in the environment-technology relationship. While *polluting* technologies generate negative environmental externalities, technological *innovation* often generates positive environmental externalities. Since industrial R&D is at least partly a public good, the private generation of technological innovations will not equal the social optimum unless public support is provided. There is no particular reason to believe that decisions taken about environmental protection taken by individual firms will necessarily take broader notions of public interest into account.[98] This is why there will continue to be a role for government in promoting environmentally-friendly technologies, even in a more globalised economy.

Thus, a convincing theoretical argument can be made for the use of a mixed regime of taxes (targeted at negative environmental externalities), and subsidies (targeted at positive technological innovations). Similar arguments can be made in other areas of the globalisation-environment relationship besides technology (Chapter 6).

Economic globalisation and the environment-intensity of technological change

According to one estimate,[99] 40% of global economic output in the first half of the 21st century will be from environment- or energy-linked products and technologies. That is one reason why Japan has created incentives for industry to develop an environmental technology "portfolio", to ensure that their technology strategies remain flexible enough to respond to increasingly unpredictable and global environmental issues, but also remain competitive in the longer-term.

If the potential benefits are so significant, why do more firms not invest sooner in environmental technology innovation? Two main obstacles seem to exist:

- *Lack of environmental expertise and information.* Many firms are simply not in a position to finance the required basic research. In a recent European survey,[100] for example, more than 75% of the firms polled requested clearer information about environmental regulations and/or available technological solutions.

- *Development costs.* Although technical solutions may be available, the cost of implementing them may be too high. When this happens, some firms – especially small and medium-sized ones – prefer to adopt a "wait-and-see" attitude.

There are influences on both the supply side (access to other factors of production) and the demand side (exposure to foreign consumption patterns) which may encourage the adoption of technologies with different environmental impacts. However, it is not certain *a priori* whether the combined effects of these two influences will be positive or negative for a particular sector, or in a particular country. For example, access to foreign technologies may displace existing domestic technologies which are better suited to local environmental conditions. Or it may allow firms to substitute less-damaging foreign equipment for more-damaging domestic machines.

As an indirect indicator of these net effects, it is interesting to compare *trade flows* in machinery and equipment with the relative stringency of environmental regulations. Data suggests[101] that the countries which are significant exporters of machinery and equipment also tend to be the countries with relatively strong regulatory regimes. Since firms are likely to develop products in line with their own regulatory requirements, this indicates that exports of capital equipment from such countries are likely to be *relatively* environmentally-benign.

This is consistent with the more general perception that increased trade may result in less- damaging production practices.[102] Although there is little empirical research to support this view, one recent examination of technological change in the pulp and paper sector found that economies which were more open to trade tended to adopt less-environmentally-damaging technologies relatively sooner (and the rate of diffusion was relatively faster) than in countries which were more closed.[103] Another study of the textile and steel sectors also found that the rate of adoption of less-damaging technologies was faster for open economies.[104] Interestingly, the greater likelihood for export-oriented firms to adopt less damaging technologies is much more pronounced for innovations related to the *product* itself (*i.e. consumption*-related environmental effects), rather than to the *process* (*i.e. production*-related environmental effects).

Most commentators also assume that international *investment flows* will result in the application of less environmentally-damaging technologies. Again, this cannot be determined *a priori*. For example, it is often argued that MNEs based in countries with strict environmental regimes will be able to draw on their experience in protecting the environment from the worst impacts of industrial activity, and will transfer this experience when they invest overseas.

The *environmental goods and services industry* is another vehicle through which environmentally-beneficial technologies might be spread. Global sales of pollution abatement equipment and related services are estimated[105] to be about $US 200 billion, of which some 90% is accounted for by OECD countries.[106] The "environment industry" has also been projected to grow by about 50% *globally* over the course of the 1990s.[107] However, observed *national* annual growth rates have varied widely, with employment in the US having grown by over 10% annually in recent years, while actually shrinking in Italy in 1993-1994.[108]

It has been estimated[109] that US trade in environmental goods and services is already in the region of 5%-10% of output. This is comparable to the pharmaceutical industry, although much lower than sectors such as automobiles and computers. Other countries, such as Finland and Norway, export as much as 50% of their output. These results partly reflect the specialised nature of much of the productive capacity which exists from country to country. For instance, of the three main exporters, Germany tends to specialise in water pollution, the United States in waste treatment and disposal, and Japan in air pollution equipment and services.

Although markets elsewhere are growing even more quickly than in OECD countries, the degree of integration with international markets varies greatly by country.[110] For instance, Brazil has by far the largest Latin American market, but a high proportion of that market is served by domestic firms. Conversely, Venezuela and Chile have much smaller markets, but import a higher proportion of their needs. The environmental industry is also becoming increasingly globalised. Thus rather than importing the technologies outright, some non-OECD countries are now turning to more integrated relationships, such as licensing and sub-contracting. This is most likely to occur in countries which have a good capacity to absorb foreign innovations.

8. CORPORATE ENVIRONMENTAL STRATEGIES[111]

The role being played by the MNEs in these changes is especially important. Since World War II, foreign direct investment by MNEs has grown faster than world international trade, and the combined sales of the world's 40 000 or so MNEs have now risen to exceed the value of world exports.[112] Some individual MNEs have grown so large that their annual turnover now surpasses the gross national products of most developing countries.[113]

There are at least three reasons for stressing the role of MNEs in the globalisation-environment interface:

- MNEs tend to be large and are therefore significant producers of pollution and/or users of natural resources.
- Because of their relatively high levels of research and development expenditures, MNEs are capable of transferring pollution abatement technologies and other environmental management practices internationally.
- MNEs often develop environmentally-friendly practices on their own, irrespective of any policy encouragement from governments. Given the dominant and growing role of the private sector in global economic activities, it is important to understand the circumstances in which these initiatives are being taken, as well as the reasons why they succeed or fail.

SMEs are also generating a significant number of environmental problems. As these firms become more global in their outlooks, these problems may intensify. Special efforts therefore need to be made to understand the environmental needs, constraints, and opportunities associated with this group. A key challenge here will be to find ways to improve the access to (and use of) *environmental information* by SMEs.

Key stakeholders in corporate environmental performance

Financial considerations continue to be the main determinant of *business* strategies among all types of company.[114] This also applies to *environmental* strategies. While the evidence is still rather sparse, it seems that 'corporate environmentalism' has so far been the strongest where "win-win" environmental opportunities have been available (strategies which simultaneously enhance both the environmental and the financial performance of the company).

This observation raises some basic concerns. First, it suggests that companies may only behave 'environmentally' when there is a profit to be made (*i.e.* preferring to ignore environmental needs when *high* abatement costs are involved). Furthermore, if environmental problems are really "external" to the polluter who creates them, we would expect the number of "win-win" opportunities to be somewhat limited (low-hanging-fruit" argument). Second, companies are not simply *presented* with "win-win" opportunities; they must expend scarce resources in locating and adapting them to their own needs. These *search costs* might rise over time, offsetting at least some of the financial benefits inherent in the original "win-win" investment.

The real challenge for corporate environmental managers, therefore, is not to pursue "win-win" strategies, but to address the more general problem of achieving environmental goals even where trade-offs are required with the company's financial performance. In thinking about these trade-offs, one important trend caused by globalisation is the increasing influence of *wider stakeholder interests* in the formulation of business strategies. These interests take the form of pressures transmitted to the company from its "multiple stakeholder" groups. They include pressures flowing from the adoption of "green" attitudes and lifestyles among individuals within those groups.

There is wide consensus[115] that, no matter what type or size of company is examined, *regulators* play a dominant role in "pushing" environmental action at the level of the firm. Two basic forces influence the relationship between MNEs and their environmental regulators. The first relates to the growing complexity of the task facing MNEs in complying with an ever-wider array of national environmental regulations. As the scope of national environmental legislation has widened, the risks associated with non-compliance have also grown. In order to control these risks, MNEs have often responded by seeking to establish closer relationships with regulators.

Tempering this "positive" view of the MNE-regulator interface is the virtual "statelessness" of many MNEs. Because they operate at a more international level, MNEs may be better able to avoid the effects of national environmental legislation by transferring some of their economic activities (*e.g.* raw materials acquisition, production activities, direct sales, demand for capital) elsewhere. As the demands of national environmental regulation increase, a shift of at least *some* MNE activity might therefore be anticipated away from countries with relatively high environmental standards, and towards those countries where environmental standards are lower ('pollution havens'). We might also expect some MNEs to attempt to use any countervailing power they have against the growing pressures exerted upon them by regulators. These issues were discussed earlier (Sections 2, 3, 4), so they are not addressed again here.

There remains considerable disagreement[116] about the impact of *"green consumerism"* on business strategies. Most evidence suggests[117] that consumers are almost as important a source of pressure on companies to pursue environmental strategies as governments and regulators. However, it is not clear whether this is due to the influence of "green consumerism" *per se*, or merely a reflection of the normal role that consumer preferences play in determining corporate strategies behaviour.

The spread of "green consumerism" has also been very uneven geographically. For example, it only really became evident in the UK in the late 1980s, by which time it was already well-established in Northern Europe (particularly in Scandinavia and Germany), where companies were already developing "green" products and marketing strategies.

Some prominent companies have also chosen to select their *trading partners* according to environmental criteria, often by developing sophisticated life cycle assessment (LCA) procedures as a screening tool. The increasing use of LCA by companies operating in consumer markets might lead to the progressive diffusion of corporate environmental management strategies further down the 'supply chain', including those companies operating in non-consumer markers. However, available evidence suggests that this approach has not yet had much influence beyond those MNEs based in countries with relatively well-developed environmental standards.[118]

For example, the German Government is presently formalising its "environmentally preferable" procurement programme for electronic office equipment – a programme inspired by the "Blue Angel" eco-labelling scheme. A similar situation is reported in the US, where the government now requires its agencies to purchase only computers that meet the energy use requirements set out under the "Energy Star" programme.[119]

However, most of the LCA methodologies adopted to date have been only "partial" in scope. For example,[120] Volkswagen Audi have used LCA informally for several years, but have tended to restrict their LCA activities to environmental impacts occurring at certain stages of the product life cycle – in particular, to the application of technologies designed to improve the fuel efficiency of the vehicle in use, as well as the recycling and re-use of certain elements of the vehicle at the disposal stage. To conduct a full LCA of their products at all stages of the product life cycle would be a virtually impossible task for this company, which produces vehicles which involve thousands of components. There is even some question about the utility of making this effort, since most of the environmental impacts associated with automobiles occur at the *consumption* stage of the life-cycle – a stage over which the MNE itself has relatively little direct control.

Nevertheless, the use of LCA practices *is* increasing.[121] For one thing, governments themselves are increasingly requiring an LCA approach. In the past, most environmental policies concentrated on environmental impacts arising during the *production* stage of the product life cycle (*e.g.* pollution emissions). During the 1990s, a new class of environmental regulations has emerged, based on the philosophy of "product stewardship". As a result, companies are increasingly being made responsible for managing the environmental impacts of their products at all stages of the product life cycle, including the sourcing of raw materials, and the ultimate disposal of the product at the end of its life. One example is the packaging "take-back" regulation introduced in Germany in 1993.

Given the greater environmental risks associated with global business strategies, we might also expect the environmental concerns of *insurers* to have considerable influence on the formulation of MNE environmental strategies. However, the evidence suggests otherwise.[122] One important reason is that the global market for pollution liability insurance has declined considerably over the past two decades Indeed, a large number of insurance companies pulled out of the pollution liability insurance market during the 1980s.

Most MNEs do *not* make extensive use of liability insurance to cover the environmental risks they face anyway. Where liability insurance *is* used, it is usually intended to cover the company only against major incidents; day-to-day environmental risks are typically borne by the company itself.

There is anecdotal evidence[123] suggesting that the kinds of pressure exerted or companies by *environmental groups* may be very significant (perhaps among the most significant faced by some companies). There are probably two reasons why globalisation is important in explaining the ever closer relationship between environmental pressure groups and companies. First, environmental problems are becoming more global themselves. This encourages environmental pressure groups to take a more global outlook.[124] Second, environmental groups are increasingly employing mass communications technologies in their campaigns (the development of satellite television and the Internet being two examples).

However, the impact of environmental interest and concern groups on corporate strategy remains very uneven. The extent to which environmental pressure groups are able to exert influence over corporations tends to depend upon a diverse range of factors, such as the degree to which the environmental issue in question is considered to be "media worthy". The media is an increasingly important vector for influencing the environmental behaviour of MNEs.

Corporate environmental responses

What *strategies* are firms employing to respond to the above-noted pressures? Some observers have suggested[125] that the reason why MNEs are demonstrating more corporate environmentalism in recent years is *ethical* (*i.e.* they accept that they have a moral responsibility to contribute to a healthy environment). However this explanation seems rather unconvincing. Rather more satisfying is an explanation that sees the environment as a route toward *long-term* profitability, even i *short-term* profits may occasionally appear to suffer.

It is possible to categorise business strategies toward the environment along three broad axes (see box). A distinction can therefore be made among: *i)* multinational firms, which are most likely to take a "proactive" approach; *ii)* large domestic

A typology of business strategies related to the environment[125]

- **"Proactive" strategies.** These firms anticipate new regulatory requirements, and react to these expected changes by seeking environmentally-friendly technological innovations which will complement their products and/or processes. They thereby try to turn new environmental restrictions into new business *opportunities*. In Europe, the proactive strategy is evident mainly among large multinational corporations, and in those industries most threatened by environmental controls (electrical utilities, chemical firms, oil refineries and water-treatment plants). This is because this strategy typically requires considerable expenditures of resources by firms.

- **"Defensive" strategies.** These include firms which view environmental restrictions as extra costs, which are to be minimised. According to a recent European survey,[126] the firms most likely to engage in defensive strategies are major companies that are leaders in their field *at home* (i.e. not multinationals), and to a lesser extent, small- and medium-sized firms. The defensive approach is most evident in the machine, textile, food-processing, wood and paper, automobile and metallurgical industries. Defensive strategies, while sometimes profitable in the short run, can expose firms to high adjustment costs if changes in standards or market conditions should occur. They can also be the cause of serious disruptions in the event of an accident. For example, prior to the (1984) Bhopal accident, Union Carbide was the world's tenth largest chemical firm. By 1994, it had fallen to 44th place.

- **"Follower" strategies.** This approach lies between the other two. For example, European manufacturers are now preparing for new guidelines in the field of waste disposal, without necessarily seeking to have these guidelines reduced ("defensive" strategy), or to profit from the new technological opportunities that they might represent ("proactive" strategy). The "follower" strategy seems to be the most popular approach overall. An estimated 55% of firms (regardless of industry) opt to deal with their environmental problems *only to the extent required by regulations*, and no more. The smaller the firm, the more pronounced this attitude becomes.

firms (probably smaller in size than the multinationals), which are more likely to adopt a "follower" strategy; and *iii)* small and medium-sized firms, which often take either a "defensive" or a "follower" posture (unless they are looking for a particular market niche).

Two basic approaches have been observed concerning how companies develop and implement these environmental strategies: the *centralised approach* and the *devolved approach*. The devolved approach implies meeting environmental standards on a country-by-country, plant-by-plant, or unit-by-unit basis. The centralised approach implies that a single set of company-wide environmental standards are applied everywhere that the MNE operates, and is roughly equivalent to what is sometimes called the "compliance plus" approach.

From an environmental perspective, the primary disadvantage of the devolved approach is that the main office of the MNE may have less control over the environmental behaviour of its individual units. This may inhibit the spread of 'good' environmental policies from high-standard countries to low-standard ones. Conversely, the devolved approach allows local business units to adapt their environmental programmes to the specific conditions in which they operate. Given that efficient environmental policies will take explicit account of local conditions, a devolved approach may eventual generate significant environmental benefits, if properly designed and implemented.

MNEs may find it advantageous to adhere to their home-based environmental standards in their overseas operations (*i.e.* the "centralised" approach) for several reasons:

- The efficiency of having a single set of management practices, pollution control technologies, and training programs geared to a common set of environmental standards may outweigh any cost advantage that might be obtained by scaling back on environmental investments at overseas facilities.

- MNEs often operate at a large scale, and recognise that their visibility makes them an especially attractive target for local enforcement officials.

- The prospect of liability for failing to meet appropriate standards often motivates better environment performance than might be required by local circumstances.

The "centralised" approach could have two other important implications for environmental policy. First, instead of representing a *threat* to national environmental policies MNEs might actually *promote* higher environmental standards, by providing a positive demonstration effect to their hosts, or by transferring environmentally-friendly technologies and organisational skills.

Second, companies would have fewer incentives to relocate their activities to low standard countries (because they would be applying similar company-wide standards wherever they operated). Clearly, the "pollution haven" hypothesis would be less of a problem in this situation.

Many companies take a "mixed" approach to their environmental strategies. For example, companies which develop LCA methodologies related to the environment sometimes generate general strategies on a company-wide basis, but then *devolve* responsibility for implementing that strategy to the individual business or site level. This is probably because developing a company-wide LCA methodology is a very difficult task, especially in highly diversified MNEs.

The *environmental audit* is an increasingly popular tool of corporate environmental management as operations become more global. Environmental audits are used in a number of different corporate contexts, and take several different forms, all of which are in fact partial in nature (in that audits typically consider only a limited part of the company's overall operations).

One reason that environmental auditing is becoming more prevalent among companies is that many have adopted some kind of *environmental management system* (EMS), which typically requires the completion of periodic environmental audits. Often, this has involved the company developing its own EMS, but companies are increasingly opting for participation in one or other of the emerging international EMS standards (such as BS7750, ISO14001 and EMAS).

The purpose of the EMS is usually to enable the company to develop its environmental strategy in a consistent and co-ordinated manner, as well as to provide a system for monitoring the company's progress towards meeting any environmental targets it has set in that strategy. However, these systems only rarely provide guidance concerning detailed environmental auditing methodologies. In effect, they commit the company to conducting regular environmental audits, but they do not prescribe how these audits should be carried out. The result is that, even though the EMS tends to be *adopted* on a centralised basis, the audit itself tends to be *carried out* on a devolved one.

Identifying what companies are doing with regard to the environment is a relatively trivial task in comparison to assessing how well they are doing it. First, there is the problem of measuring corporate environmental performance. Second, there is the problem of evaluating what has been measured. Another complication is that while many MNEs now publish data on various aspects of their environmental performance, there has been very little *ex post* evaluation of corporate environmental performance (leaving aside the issue of the reliability of this data). There is thus a glaring need for better evaluations of corporate environmental behaviour, and for the data upon which such evaluations might be based.[127]

9.   FUTURE DIRECTIONS FOR THE OECD

Section 2 discussed the "leadership vacuum" that is becoming increasingly evident in the environmental response to economic globalisation. It also noted the potential role that key regional economic bodies might make toward filling this vacuum.

The OECD is one of these key regional economic bodies.[128] It also has routine linkages with the other main country group in the globalisation-environment relationship – the developing countries. Furthermore, it is in regular contact with the business, labour, and environmental non-governmental communities, all of which have a stake in globalisation-environment issues.

The OECD is therefore in an excellent position to provide some of the leadership currently lacking on globalisation-environment questions. Indeed, it is already moving in this direction in some areas (*e.g.* the ongoing negotiations toward a Multilateral Agreement on Investments are currently examining how environmental concerns might best be incorporated).

However, the *environmental* side of the globalisation-environment linkage needs to be more fully developed, and this is where OECD countries could make their most significant additional contribution to the debate. More specifically, two broad priorities are suggested:

- *Analyse* (both quantitatively and qualitatively) specific elements of the globalisation-environment relationship. *Quantitative empirical evidence* is currently lacking on virtually all components of this relationship. The amount of *environmental risk* associated with various globalisation scenarios, as well as the *optimum levels of government response* to these risks, should be a key part of any such analyses.

- Provide a *forum* and serve as a *catalyst* for *new co-operative international initiatives* aimed at reducing tensions in the globalisation-environment relationship (see Section 2 for potential examples).

NOTES

1. See Jones (1997).
2. Luttwack (1996).
3. OECD (1991).
4. OECD (1996e).
5. Pitchon (1995).
6. Goldsmith (1995).
7. For recent examples, see OECD (1991); (1993); (1994); (1995a); and (1996 a, b, c, d).
8. OECD (1996e).
9. See Gerrelli (1996).
10. See, for example, Seldon and Song (1994).
11. For example, see Campbell (1993).
12. See Zarsky (1997) and Gerelli (1997).
13. Williamson (1996) and O'Rourke and Williamson (1995).
14. See Adams (1997a).
15. Repetto (1995).
16. Hitchens *et al.* (1996).
17. Gray and Shadbegian (1993) and (1995).
18. US Congress (1994), Table A-1, p. 323.
19. Management Institute for Environment and Business (1995).
20. See Kalt (1988) and more recently, Han and Braden (1996).
21. For example, see Grossman and Krueger (1992); and Tobey (1989).
22. See Sorsa (1994) and Low and Yeats (1992).
23. See Esty and Gentry (1997).
24. World Bank (1996).
25. Esty and Gentry (1997) and UNCTAD (1996).
26. Esty and Mendelsohn (1995).
27. Esty and Mendelsohn (1995).

28. Gentry and Fernandez (1996).
29. See Esty and Gentry (1997).
30. Esty and Mendelsohn (1995).
31. See Adams (1997a).
32. Benedickson *et al.* (1994).
33. Repetto (1995).
34. See Dasgupta, Mody and Singh (1995).
35. USTR (1992).
36. For example, see Xing and Kolstad (1996).
37. Gentry and Fernandez (1996).
38. Gentry and Fernandez (1996).
39. Esty (1995) and Gentry (1997).
40. World Bank (1996) and ADB (1993).
41. Gentry and Fernandez (1996).
42. Gentry and Fernandez (1996).
43. Gentry (1996).
44. Esty (1997).
45. See Adams (1997b) and Schleicher (1997).
46. See WTO (1995).
47. See OECD (1994), OECD (1995c), and Johnstone (1996).
48. OECD (1995c).
49. For example, see Birdsall and Wheeler (1993).
50. WTO/CTE (1996) and OECD (1995c).
51. See Jones and Youngman (1997).
52. Based on OECD (1996i) and IEA (1995).
53. Based on Burtraw *et al.* (1996).
54. Based on IEA (1995).
55. Based on personal communications with IEA staff. See Jones and Youngman (1997).
56. CERA (1995).
57. Based on IEA (1996).
58. Personal communication, Ted Button, WBCSD (World Business Council on Sustainable Development).
59. Based on OECD (1996h) and OECD (1997).
60. See OECD (1996h).
61. OECD (1997).
62. OECD (1996m).

63. Greene (1996), p. 144.
64. Based on Reynaud (1996).
65. Repetto (1995).
66. Anderson and Strutt (1994).
67. See OECD (1995c).
68. OECD (1996k).
69. OECD (1996j).
70. See Anderson and Strutt (1994).
71. See OECD (1995b).
72. OECD (1995b).
73. OECD (1995b).
74. OECD (1996k).
75. See Johnstone (1997) and Faucheux, O'Connor, and Nicolai (1997).
76. Coe and Helpman (1995).
77. Archibugi and Michie (1995).
78. OECD (1995a), p. 63.
79. Coe and Helpman (1995), p. 862.
80. UN (1996), Table A-17.
81. Archibugi and Michie (1995), pp. 130-134.
82. Freeman and Hagedoorn (1995), p. 51.
83. See Abramovitz (1994).
84. See, for example, Romer (1989), Scott (1989), and Grossman and Helpman (1991).
85. See Dosi et al. (1990).
86. See Blomstrom and Kokko (1996), p. 33.
87. See Fagerberg (1994), p. 1161.
88. Rosseger (1996).
89. See Hikino and Amsdem (1994).
90. Young and Sachs (1995), p. 80.
91. See OECD (1995a).
92. Calculated on the basis of USDOC PACE (1993) and (1996).
93. For example, see Henriques and Sadorsky (1996).
94. See Kemp et al. (1992) and Kemp and Soete (1990).
95. Nentjes and Wiersma (1987), p. 64.
96. Vogan (1996), Chart 2.
97. Jaffe and Stavins (1994).
98. Among others, see Ferrante (1996).

99. MITI (1988); Miller and Moore (1994); and Erkman (1996).

100. European Commission (1995).

101. OECD (1996g).

102. Among others, see Beghin et al. (1995); and Birdsall and Wheeler (1993).

103. Among others, see Wheeler and Martin (1992).

104. Blackman and Boyd (1995).

105. Duchin et al. (1995).

106. OECD (1992).

107. OECD (1992).

108. OECD (1996f).

109. OECD (1996f).

110. OECD (1996f).

111. See Garrod (1997).

112. Dunning (1996).

113. Griffiths and Wall (1991).

114. Steadman, Zimmerer and Green (1995).

115. For example, see Peattie and Ringler (1994).

116. For examples, see Garrod and Chadwick (1996).

117. Welford and Gouldson (1993).

118. Barry (1990).

119. See Dirksen (1996) and Bast (1994).

120. See Gouldson (1994).

121. See Bast (1994) and (1996).

122. See Steiner and Steiner (1994).

123. For example, see the debate between Greenpeace International and Shell Oil, concerning disposal of the Brent spar oil rig.

124. Caldwell (1991).

125. Steiner and Steiner (1994).

126. See Faucheux, O'Connor and Nicolai (1997).

127. European Commission (1995).

128. This subject is currently under consideration by the OECD Industry Committee.

129. It is "regional" in the sense that it encompasses most of the world's developed economies; it is "economic" in the sense that its mandate includes economic cooperation and development.

REFERENCES

ABRAMOVITZ, MOSES (1994). "Catch-Up and Convergence in the Post-War Growth Boom and After". In W. J. BAUMOL *ET AL.* (eds). *Convergence of Productivity: Cross-National Studies and Historical Evidence.* OUP: Oxford.

ADAMS, JAN (1997a). "Environmental Policy and Competitiveness in a Globalised Economy: Conceptual Issues and a Review of the Empirical Evidence". Draft paper prepared for a Workshop on Economic Globalisation and the Environment, Vienna (January 30-31).

ADAMS, JAN (1997b). "Globalisation, Trade and Environment". Draft paper prepared for a Workshop on Economic Globalisation and the Environment, Vienna (January 30-31).

ADB (ASIAN DEVELOPMENT BANK) (1993). *Environmental Guidelines for Selected Industrial and Power Development Projects.* ADB: Manila.

ANDERSON, KYM AND ANNA STRUTT (1994). *On Measuring the Environmental Impacts of Agricultural Trade Liberalization.* University of Adelaide, Centre for International Economic Studies, Seminar Paper 94-06: Adelaide Australia.

ARCHIBUGI, DANIELE AND JONATHAN MICHIE (1995). "The Globalisation of Technology: A New Taxonomy". *Cambridge Journal of Economics*, Vol. 19, pp. 121-140.

BARRY, T. (1990). "Are Buyers Going Green?" *Purchasing and Supply Management.* May, pp. 27-29.

BAST, C. (1994). "Hewlett Packard's Approach to Creating a Life-Cycle (Product Stewardship Program". *International Symposium on Electronics and the Environment: Hewlett Packard's Proceedings*, San Francisco, March 2-3.

BAST, C. (1996). "Hewlett Packard's Self-Assessment Procedure for Product Stewardship". *International Symposium on Electronics and the Environment: Hewlett Packard's Proceedings*, Dallas, May 6-8.

BEGHIN, J., D. ROLAND-HOLST AND D. VAN DER MENSBRUGGHE (1995). "Trade Liberalisation and the Environment in the Pacific Basin: Co-ordinated Approaches to Mexican Trade and Environment Policy". *American Journal of Agricultural Economics*, Vol. 77 (August), pp. 778-785.

BENEDICKSON, J.G. B. DOERN, AND NANCY OLEWILER (1994). *Getting the Green Light: Environmental Regulation and Investment in Canada.* Policy Study No. 22, C.D. Howe Institute: Toronto.

BIRDSALL, N. AND D. WHEELER (1993). "Trade Policy and Industrial Pollution in Latin America: Where are the Pollution Havens?" *Journal of Environment and Development*, Vol. 2, No. 1 (Winter).

BLACKMAN, ALLEN AND JAMES BOYD (1995). "The Usefulness of Macroeconomic Statistics in Explaining International Differences in the Diffusion of Process Innovations". *Resources for the Future Discussion Paper 95-10:* Washington, DC

BLOMSTROM, MAGNUS AND ARI KOKKO (1996). "Multinational Corporations and Spillovers". *CEPR Discussion Paper* No. 1365: London.

BURTRAW, DALLAS, A. KRUPNICK, AND K. PALMER (1996). "Air Quality and Electricity: What Competition May Mean". *Resources*, 123 (Spring).

CALDWELL, L.K. (1991). "Globalizing Environmentalism: Threshold of a New Phase in International Relations". *Society and Natural Resources*, Vol. 4, No. 3, pp. 259-272.

CAMBRIDGE ENERGY RESEARCH ASSOCIATES (CERA) (1995). "Sizing Up: The International Private Power Market". Special Report Overview: Cambridge, MA.

CAMPBELL, BRUCE (1993). "Globalisation, Trade Agreements, and Sustainability". In CANADIAN ENVIRONMENTAL LAW ASSOCIATION. *The Environmental Implications of Trade Agreements.* Queen's Printer: Toronto.

COE, DAVID T. (1995). "North-South R&D Spillovers". *CEPR Discussion Paper* No. 1133: London.

COE, DAVID T. AND ELHANAN HELPMAN (1995). "International R&D Spillovers". *European Economic Review*, Vol. 39, pp. 859-887.

DASGUPTA, SUSMITA, ASHOKA MODY AND SARBAJIT SINHA (1995). *Japanese Multinationals in Asia: Capabilities and Motivations.* World Bank: Washington DC.

DIRKSEN, T. (1996). "Hewlett Packard's Experience with the German Blue Angel Eco-label". *International Symposium on Electronics and the Environment: Hewlett Packard's Proceedings*, Dallas, May 6-8.

DOSI, G. ET AL. (1990). *The Economics of Technological Change and International Trade.* Harvester Wheatsheaf: London.

DUCHIN, FAYE ET AL. (1995). "Technological Change, Trade and the Environment". *Ecological Economics*, Vol. 14, pp. 185-193.

DUNNING, J.H. (1996). "Globalisation, Foreign Direct Investment and Economic Development". *Economics and Business Education*, Vol. 4, No. 2, Summer, pp. 46-51.

ERKMAN, S. (1996). "Industrial Ecology: A Historical View". *Journal of Cleaner Production*, December.

ESTY, DANIEL C. (1995). "Private Sector Foreign Investment and the Environment". *Review of European Community and International Environmental Law*, Vol. 4, No. 2.

ESTY, DANIEL C. AND ROBERT MENDELSOHN(1995). *Powering China: The Environmental Implications of China's Economic Growth.* Yale Center for Environmental Law and Policy: New Haven.

ESTY, DANIEL C. AND BRADFORD GENTRY (1997). "Foreign Investment, Globalisation and the Environment". Draft paper prepared for a Workshop on Economic Globalisation and the Environment, Vienna (January 30-31).

EUROPEAN COMMISSION (DG III) (1995). *Attitude and Strategy of Business Regarding Protection of the Environment: Common Environmental Framework.* European Commission: Brussels.

FAGERBERG, JAN (1994). "Technology and International Differences in Growth Rates". *Journal of Economic Literature*, Vol. 32, pp. 1147-1175.

FAUCHEUX, SYLVIE, MARTIN O'CONNOR AND ISABELLE NICOLAI (1997). Economic Globalisation, Competitiveness and Environment". Draft paper prepared for a Workshop on Economic Globalisation and the Environment, Vienna (January 30-31).

FERRANTE, FANCESCO (1996). "Does History Matter? Localised Scientific Advance, Missing Markets for the Environment and the Efficient Control of Pollution". University of Cassino, Department of Economics (mimeo).

FREEMAN, CHRIS AND JOHN HAGEDOORN (1995). "Convergence and Divergence in the Internationalisation of Technology". In JOHN HAGEDOORN (ED.). *Technical Change in the World Economy.* Edward Elgar: London.

GARROD, BRIAN (1997). "Business Strategies, Globalisation and the Environment". Draft paper prepared for a Workshop on Economic Globalisation and the Environment, Vienna (January 30-31).

GARROD, B. AND P. CHADWICK. (1996). "Environmental Management and Business Strategy: Towards a New Strategic Paradigm?" *Futures*, Vol. 28, No. 1, pp. 37-50.

GENTRY, BRADFORD S. (1997). *Making Private Finance Work for the Environment.* United Nations Development Program, Office of Development Studies Discussion Paper.

GENTRY, BRADFORD S. AND LISA FERNANDEZ (1996*). Survey on Corporate Valuation and the Environment.* United Nations Development Program, Office of Development Studies Discussion Paper (draft).

GERELLI, EMILIO (1996). "Post-Industrial Society and the Environment". Manuscript.

GERELLI, EMILIO (1997). "Environmental Governance in the Global Village". Draft paper prepared for a Workshop on Economic Globalisation and the Environment, Vienna (January 30-31).

GOLDSMITH, JAMES (1995). "Turbo-Charged Capitalism is the Enemy of Family Values". *International Herald Tribune.*

GOULDSON, A. (1994). "Life-Cycle Environmental Management and Product Innovation: The Case of the Volkswagen Audi Group". In R. WELFORD. *Cases in Environmental Management and Business Strategy.* Pitman: London.

GRAY, WAYNE B. AND RONALD SHADBEGIAN (1993). "Environmental Regulation and Manufacturing Productivity at the Plant Level". *National Bureau of Economic Research Working Paper* No. 4321.

GRAY, WAYNE B. AND RONALD SHADBEGIAN (1995). "Pollution Abatement Costs, Regulation, and Plant-Level Productivity". *National Bureau of Economic Research Working Paper* No. 4994.

GREENE, DAVID L. (1996). *Transportation and Energy.* ENO Transportation Foundation, Inc.: Landsdowne, VA.

GRIFFITHS, A. AND S. WALL (1991). *Applied Economics: An Introductory Course* (4th Edition). Longman: London.

GROSSMAN, GENE M. AND ELHANAN HELPMAN (1991). *Innovation and Growth in the Global Economy.* MIT Press: Cambridge, Mass.

GROSSMAN, GENE M AND ALAN B. KRUEGER (1992). "Environmental Impacts of a North American Free Trade Agreement". *Centre for Economic Policy Research Discussion Paper* No 644: London.

HAN, KI-JU AND JOHN B. BRADEN (1996). "Environment and Trade: New Evidence from US Manufacturing". Unpublished research paper, Department of Economics, University of Illinois and Department of Agriculture and Consumer Economics: University of Urbana-Champaign.

HENRIQUES, IRENE AND PERRY SADORSKY (1996). "The Determinants of an Environmentally Responsive Firm: An Empirical Approach". *Journal of Environmental Economics and Management*, Vol. 30, pp. 381-395.

HIKINO, TAKASHI AND ALICE H. AMSDEM (1994). "Staying Behind, Stumbling Back, Sneaking Up, Soaring Ahead: Late Industrialisation in Historical Perspective". In W. J. BAUMOL ET AL. (EDS.). *Convergence of Productivity: Cross-National Studies and Historical Evidence.* OUP: Oxford.

HITCHENS, D.M.W.N. ET AL. (1996). *Effects on Employment Skills, Productivity and Competitiveness of Environmental Regulation in Food Processing Across the EU.* European Foundation Working Paper.

INTERNATIONAL ENERGY AGENCY (1995). "Inter-system Competition and Trade in Electricity – Implications for the Environment and Environmental Policy". Restricted paper IEA/SLT(95)25, prepared for the IEA Standing Group on Long-Term Co-operation.

INTERNATIONAL ENERGY AGENCY (1996). *World Energy Outlook, 1996 Edition.* OECD Paris.

JAFFE, ADAM B. AND ROBERT N. STAVINS (1994). "Environmental Regulation and Technology Diffusion: The Effects of Alternative Policy Instruments". *Resources for the Future Discussion Paper* (94-38): Washington, DC.

JOHNSTONE, NICK (1996). "The Environment and Linkage-Intensive Development." Draft paper prepared for OECD Environment Directorate Linkages II project.

JOHNSTONE, NICK (1997). "Globalisation, Technology and Environment". Draft paper prepared for a Workshop on Economic Globalisation and the Environment, Vienna (January 30-31).

JONES, TOM (1997). "Globalisation and Environment: Main Issues". Draft paper prepared for a Workshop on Economic Globalisation and the Environment, Vienna (January 30-31).

JONES, TOM AND ROB YOUNGMAN (1997). "Globalisation and Environment: Selected Sectoral Issues". Draft paper prepared for a Workshop on Economic Globalisation and the Environment, Vienna (January 30-31).

KALT, JOSEPH P. (1988). "The Impact of Domestic Environmental Regulatory Policies on US International Competitiveness. " *International Competitiveness.* Harper and Row, Ballinger: Cambridge, MA.

KEMP, RENE *ET AL.* (1992). "Supply and Demand Factors of Cleaner Technologies". *Environmental and Resource Economics,* Vol. 2, pp. 615-634.

KEMP, RENE AND L. SOETE (1990). "Inside the "Green Box": On the Economics of Technological Change and the Environment". In C. FREEMAN AND L. SOETE (EDS.). *New Exploration in the Economics of Technical Change.* Pinter: London.

LOW, PATRICK (ED.) (1992). *International Trade and the Environment.* World Bank Discussion Paper 159: Washington, DC.

LOW, PATRICK AND ALEXANDER YEATS (1992). "Do "Dirty" Industries Migrate?" In P. LOW (1992) *supra,* pp 89-103.

LUTTWACK, EDWARD (1996). "Who has a Political Cure for Turbo-Capitalism?" *International Herald Tribune.*

MANAGEMENT INSTITUTE FOR ENVIRONMENT AND BUSINESS (1995). *Competitive Implications of Environmental Regulation* (various case studies prepared for the Office of Policy, Planning and Evaluation). US Environmental Protection Agency: Washington, DC.

MILLER A. AND C. MOORE (1994). "Strengths and Limitation of Governmental Support for Environmental Technology in Japan". *Industrial and Environmental Crisis Quarterly,* 8, 2, pp. 155-170.

MITI (1988). "Trends and Future Tasks in Industrial Technology. Developing Innovative Technologies to Support the 21st Century". Summary of the White Paper on Industrial Technology, 29 pages, September.

NENTJES, ANDRIES AND DOEDE WIERSMA (1987). "Innovation and Pollution Control". *International Journal of Social Economics,* Vol. 15, pp. 51-71.

OECD (1991). *Globalisation and Regionalisation.* OECD: Paris.

OECD (1992). *The OECD Environment Industry: Situation, Prospects and Government Policies.* OECD: Paris.

OECD (1993). *Environmental Policies and Industrial Competitiveness.* OECD: Paris.

OECD (1994). *The Environmental Effects of Trade.* OECD: Paris.

OECD (1995a). *Technologies for Cleaner Production and Products.* OECD: Paris.

OECD (1995b). *Sustainable Agriculture: Concepts, Issues and Policies in OECD Countries.* OECD: Paris.

OECD (1995c). *Report on Trade and Environment to the OECD Council at Ministerial Level.* OECD: Paris.

OECD (1996a). "Globalisation of Economic Activities and its Implications for International Aviation". Restricted report SG/AU/AT(95)5/REV1.

OECD (1996b). *Integrating Environment and Economy: Progress in the 1990s*. OECD: Paris.

OECD (1996c). *Globalisation and Competitiveness: Relevant Indicators*. OECD: Paris.

OECD (1996d). *Globalisation: What Challenges and Opportunities for Governments?* OECD: Paris.

OECD (1996e). *Communiqué Issued Following the May 21-21, 1996 Meeting of the OECD Council at Ministerial Level*. OECD: Paris.

OECD (1996f). *The Environmental Goods and Services Industry*. OECD: Paris.

OECD (1996g). *The OECD in Figures*. OECD: Paris.

OECD (1996h). "Liberalization in the Transportation Sector in North America". Restricted paper COM/TD/ENV(96)71, prepared for the OECD Joint Session of Trade and Environment Experts.

OECD (1996i). "The Economy-Wide Effects of Regulatory Reform". Restricted paper ECO/GEN(96)15, with accompanying "Country Notes" ECO/GEN(96)15/ANN, prepared as background material for the 1997 OECD Ministerial meeting.

OECD (1996j). *Agricultural Policies, Markets and Trade in OECD Countries: Monitoring and Evaluation (1996)*. OECD: Paris.

OECD (1996k). "Agriculture, Trade and the Environment: Anticipating the Policy Challenges". Restricted paper COM/AGR/CA/ENV/EPOC(96)148 prepared for the Joint Working Party of the Committee for Agriculture and the Environment Policy Committee.

OECD (1996l). "The Environmental Effects of Freight Transport". Restricted Document COM/TD/ENV(96)72, prepared for the Joint Session of Trade and Environment Experts.

OECD (1996m). "Trade Liberalisation and Changes in International Freight Movements". Restricted paper COM/TD/ENV(96)73, prepared for the OECD Joint Session of Trade and Environment Experts.

OECD (1997). "Liberalisation and Structural Reform in the Freight Transport Sector in Europe". Restricted paper COM/TD/ENV(97)11, prepared for the Joint Session of Trade and Environment Experts.

O'ROURKE, K.H. AND J.G. WILLIAMSON (1995). "Around the European Periphery 1870-1913: Globalisation, Schooling and Growth". *National Bureau of Economic Research Working Paper* No. 5392: Cambridge, Mass.

PEARSON, CHARLES S. (1987). *Multinational Corporations, Environment, and the Third World*. Duke University Press : Durham, North Carolina (pp. 3-31).

PEATTIE, K. AND A. RINGLER. (1994). 'Management and the Environment in the UK and Germany: A Comparison'. *European Management Journal*, Vol. 12, No. 2, pp. 216-225.

PITCHON, PATRICIA (1995). "The Unemployed: A North-South Dilemma". *Share International*, October.

REPETTO, ROBERT. (1995). *Jobs, Competitiveness and Environmental Regulation: What Are the Real Issues?*. World Resources Institute: Washington, DC.

REPETTO, ROBERT, DALE ROTHMAN, PAUL FAETH, AND DUNCAN AUSTIN (1996). *Has Environmental Protection Really Reduced Economic Productivity?* World Resources Institute: Washington, DC.

REYNAUD, CHRISTIAN (1996). "Latest Trends in Transport in Central and Eastern Europe". In ECMT. *Access to European Transport Markets*. OECD: Paris.

ROMER, P. M. (1989). "What Determines the Rate of Growth and Technical Change?" *World Bank Planning and Research Paper*, No. WPS 279.

ROSSEGER, G. (1996). *The Economics of Production and Innovation*. Butterworth Heinemann: London.

SCHLEICHER, STEPHAN (1997). "Borders to Trade in a Borderless World". Draft paper prepared for a Workshop on Economic Globalisation and the Environment, Vienna (January 30-31).

SCOTT, M. (1989). *A New View of Economic Growth*. OUP: Oxford.

SELDEN, THOMAS AND D. SONG (1994). "Environmental Quality and Development: Is There a Kuznets Curve for Air Emissions?" *Journal of Environmental Economics and Management*, 27, 2, pp. 147-162.

SORSA, PIRITTA (1994). "Competitiveness and Environmental Standards: Some Exploratory Results". *Policy Research Working Paper* 1249. World Bank: Washington, DC.

STEADMAN, M.E., T.W. ZIMMERER, AND R.F. GREEN (1995). "Pressures From Stakeholders Hit Japanese Companies". *Long Range Planning*, Vol. 28, No. 6, pp. 29-37.

STEINER, G.A. AND F.J. STEINER. (1994). *Business, Government, and Society: A Managerial Perspective: Text and Cases* (7th Edition): McGraw Hill International.

TOBEY, JAMES A. (1989). "The Effects of Domestic Environmental Policies on Patterns of World Trade: An Empirical Test". *Kyklos*, Vol. 43, No. 2, pp. 191-209.

UNCTAD (UNITED NATIONS CONFERENCE ON TRADE AND DEVELOPMENT) (1996). *World Investment Report (1996): Investment, Trade, and International Policy Arrangements*. UNCTAD: Geneva.

UNITED NATIONS (1996). *World Economic and Social Survey*. UN: New York:

UNITED STATES DEPARTMENT OF COMMERCE (1996). *Pollution Abatement Costs and Expenditures: 1994*. USGPO: Washington, DC.

US CONGRESS OTA (1994). "Industry, Technology and the Environment: Competitive Challenges and Business Opportunities: US Govt Printing Case of US Firms". *Journal of International Economics*, Vol. 33, pp. 57-76.

USTR (UNITED STATES TRADE REPRESENTATIVE) (1992). *Review of US-Mexico Environmental Issues*.

VOGAN, CHRISTINE R. (1996). "Pollution Abatement and Control Expenditures: 1972-1994". *Survey of Current Business*, September 1996.

WELFORD, R. AND A. GOULDSON. (1993). *Environmental Management and Business Strategy*. Pitman: London.

WHEELER, DAVID AND PAUL MARTIN (1992). "Prices, Policies and the International Diffusion of Clean Technology: The Case of Wood Pulp Production". In P. LOW (ed.). (1992), *supra*.

WILLIAMSON, J.G. (1996). "Globalisation and Inequality: Then and Now – The Late 19th and Late 20th Centuries Compared". *National Bureau of Economic Research Working Paper* No. 5491: Cambridge, MA.

WORLD BANK (1996). *World Debt Tables (1996)*. World Bank: Washington,

WTO (1995). *International Trade: Trends and Statistics*. World Trade Organisation: Geneva.

WTO/CTE (1996). "Report (1996) of the Committee on Trade and Environment". Restricted document WT/CTE/W/40, 7 November.

XING, YUQING AND CHARLES D. KOLSTAD (1996). *Do Lax Environmental Regulations Attract Foreign Investment?*. Paper presented to the National Bureau of Economic Research. Workshop on Public Policy and the Environment: Cambridge, Mass.

YOUNG, JOHN E. AND AARON SACHS (1995). "Creating a Sustainable Materials Economy". In LESTER BROWN *ET AL.* (EDS.). *State of the World 1995*. London: Earthscan.

ZARSKY, LYUBA (1997). "Stuck in the Mud? Management Issues in the Globalisation/Environment Relationship". Draft paper prepared for a Workshop on Economic Globalisation and the Environment, Vienna (January 30-31).

MAIN SALES OUTLETS OF OECD PUBLICATIONS
PRINCIPAUX POINTS DE VENTE DES PUBLICATIONS DE L'OCDE

AUSTRALIA – AUSTRALIE
D.A. Information Services
648 Whitehorse Road, P.O.B 163
Mitcham, Victoria 3132   Tel. (03) 9210.7777
                         Fax: (03) 9210.7788

AUSTRIA – AUTRICHE
Gerold & Co.
Graben 31
Wien I   Tel. (0222) 533.50.14
                    Fax: (0222) 512.47.31.29

BELGIUM – BELGIQUE
Jean De Lannoy
Avenue du Roi, Koningslaan 202
B-1060 Bruxelles Tel. (02) 538.51.69/538.08.41
                         Fax: (02) 538.08.41

CANADA
Renouf Publishing Company Ltd.
5369 Canotek Road
Unit 1
Ottawa, Ont. K1J 9J3   Tel. (613) 745.2665
                         Fax: (613) 745.7660
Stores:
71 1/2 Sparks Street
Ottawa, Ont. K1P 5R1   Tel. (613) 238.8985
                         Fax: (613) 238.6041
12 Adelaide Street West
Toronto, QN M5H 1L6   Tel. (416) 363.3171
                         Fax: (416) 363.5963
Les Éditions La Liberté Inc.
3020 Chemin Sainte-Foy
Sainte-Foy, PQ G1X 3V6 Tel. (418) 658.3763
                         Fax: (418) 658.3763
Federal Publications Inc.
165 University Avenue, Suite 701
Toronto, ON M5H 3B8   Tel. (416) 860.1611
                         Fax: (416) 860.1608
Les Publications Fédérales
1185 Université
Montréal, QC H3B 3A7   Tel. (514) 954.1633
                         Fax: (514) 954.1635

CHINA – CHINE
Book Dept., China Natinal Publications
Import and Export Corporation (CNPIEC)
16 Gongti E. Road, Chaoyang District
Beijing 100020 Tel. (10) 6506-6688 Ext. 8402
                         (10) 6506-3101

CHINESE TAIPEI – TAIPEI CHINOIS
Good Faith Worldwide Int'l. Co. Ltd.
9th Floor, No. 118, Sec. 2
Chung Hsiao E. Road
Taipei   Tel. (02) 391.7396/391.7397
                         Fax: (02) 394.9176

**CZECH REPUBLIC –
RÉPUBLIQUE TCHÈQUE**
National Information Centre
NIS – prodejna
Konviktská 5
Praha 1 – 113 57   Tel. (02) 24.23.09.07
                    Fax: (02) 24.22.94.33
E-mail: nkposp@dec.niz.cz
Internet: http://www.nis.cz

DENMARK – DANEMARK
Munksgaard Book and Subscription Service
35, Nørre Søgade, P.O. Box 2148
DK-1016 København K   Tel. (33) 12.85.70
                         Fax: (33) 12.93.87
J. H. Schultz Information A/S,
Herstedvang 12,
DK – 2620 Albertslung   Tel. 43 63 23 00
                         Fax: 43 63 19 69
Internet: s-info@inet.uni-c.dk

EGYPT – ÉGYPTE
The Middle East Observer
41 Sherif Street
Cairo   Tel. (2) 392.6919
                         Fax: (2) 360.6804

FINLAND – FINLANDE
Akateeminen Kirjakauppa
Keskuskatu 1, P.O. Box 128
00100 Helsinki

Subscription Services/Agence d'abonnements :
P.O. Box 23
00100 Helsinki   Tel. (358) 9.121.4403
                         Fax: (358) 9.121.4450

*FRANCE
OECD/OCDE
Mail Orders/Commandes par correspondance :
2, rue André-Pascal
75775 Paris Cedex 16 Tel. 33 (0)1.45.24.82.00
                    Fax: 33 (0)1.49.10.42.76
                    Telex: 640048 OCDE
Internet: Compte.PUBSINQ@oecd.org

Orders via Minitel, France only/
Commandes par Minitel, France
exclusivement : 36 15 OCDE

OECD Bookshop/Librairie de l'OCDE :
33, rue Octave-Feuillet
75016 Paris   Tel. 33 (0)1.45.24.81.81
                         33 (0)1.45.24.81.67
Dawson
B.P. 40
91121 Palaiseau Cedex   Tel. 01.89.10.47.00
                         Fax: 01.64.54.83.26
Documentation Française
29, quai Voltaire
75007 Paris   Tel. 01.40.15.70.00
Economica
49, rue Héricart
75015 Paris   Tel. 01.45.78.12.92
                         Fax: 01.45.75.05.67
Gibert Jeune (Droit-Économie)
6, place Saint-Michel
75006 Paris   Tel. 01.43.25.91.19
Librairie du Commerce International
10, avenue d'Iéna
75016 Paris   Tel. 01.40.73.34.60
Librairie Dunod
Université Paris-Dauphine
Place du Maréchal-de-Lattre-de-Tassigny
75016 Paris   Tel. 01.44.05.40.13
Librairie Lavoisier
11, rue Lavoisier
75008 Paris   Tel. 01.42.65.39.95
Librairie des Sciences Politiques
30, rue Saint-Guillaume
75007 Paris   Tel. 01.45.48.36.02
P.U.F.
49, boulevard Saint-Michel
75005 Paris   Tel. 01.43.25.83.40
Librairie de l'Université
12a, rue Nazareth
13100 Aix-en-Provence   Tel. 04.42.26.18.08
Documentation Française
165, rue Garibaldi
69003 Lyon   Tel. 04.78.63.32.23
Librairie Decitre
29, place Bellecour
69002 Lyon   Tel. 04.72.40.54.54
Librairie Sauramps
Le Triangle
34967 Montpellier Cedex 2 Tel. 04.67.58.85.15
                         Fax: 04.67.58.27.36
A la Sorbonne Actual
23, rue de l'Hôtel-des-Postes
06000 Nice   Tel. 04.93.13.77.75
                         Fax: 04.93.80.75.69

GERMANY – ALLEMAGNE
OECD Bonn Centre
August-Bebel-Allee 6
D-53175 Bonn   Tel. (0228) 959.120
                         Fax: (0228) 959.12.17

GREECE – GRÈCE
Librairie Kauffmann
Stadiou 28
10564 Athens   Tel. (01) 32.55.321
                         Fax: (01) 32.30.320

HONG-KONG
Swindon Book Co. Ltd.
Astoria Bldg. 3F
34 Ashley Road, Tsimshatsui
Kowloon, Hong Kong   Tel. 2376.2062
                         Fax: 2376.0685

HUNGARY – HONGRIE
Euro Info Service
Margitsziget, Európa Ház
1138 Budapest   Tel. (1) 111.60.61
                         Fax: (1) 302.50.35
E-mail: euroinfo@mail.matav.hu
Internet: http://www.euroinfo.hu//index.html

ICELAND – ISLANDE
Mál og Menning
Laugavegi 18, Pósthólf 392
121 Reykjavik   Tel. (1) 552.4240
                         Fax: (1) 562.3523

INDIA – INDE
Oxford Book and Stationery Co.
Scindia House
New Delhi 110001   Tel. (11) 331.5896/5308
                         Fax: (11) 332.2639
E-mail: oxford.publ@axcess.net.in
17 Park Street
Calcutta 700016   Tel. 240832

INDONESIA – INDONÉSIE
Pdii-Lipi
P.O. Box 4298
Jakarta 12042   Tel. (21) 573.34.67
                         Fax: (21) 573.34.67

IRELAND – IRLANDE
Government Supplies Agency
Publications Section
4/5 Harcourt Road
Dublin 2   Tel. 661.31.11
                         Fax: 475.27.60

ISRAEL – ISRAËL
Praedicta
5 Shatner Street
P.O. Box 34030
Jerusalem 91430   Tel. (2) 652.84.90/1/2
                         Fax: (2) 652.84.93
R.O.Y. International
P.O. Box 13056
Tel Aviv 61130   Tel. (3) 546 1423
                         Fax: (3) 546 1442
E-mail: royil@netvision.net.il
Palestinian Authority/Middle East:
INDEX Information Services
P.O.B. 19502
Jerusalem   Tel. (2) 627.16.34
                         Fax: (2) 627.12.19

ITALY – ITALIE
Libreria Commissionaria Sansoni
Via Duca di Calabria, 1/1
50125 Firenze   Tel. (055) 64.54.15
                         Fax: (055) 64.12.57
E-mail: licosa@ftbcc.it
Via Bartolini 29
20155 Milano   Tel. (02) 36.50.83
Editrice e Libreria Herder
Piazza Montecitorio 120
00186 Roma   Tel. 679.46.28
                         Fax: 678.47.51